Grow Your Happiness

Grow Your Happiness:

How 10 Minutes a Day Can Help You Feel Better (and Better) in Life

Rex Basham

Grow Your Happiness: How 10 Minutes a Day Can Help You Feel Better (and Better) in Life

Copyright © 2020 by Rex Basham

Published by Rex Basham
www.ToolsForFeelingBetter.com

Editors: Karen Williams, Josephine Ferguson, Mary Scott
Cover Design: Danielle Smith-Boldt
Internal Layout: Rex Basham

All rights reserved. No part of this publication may be reproduced, distributed, or transmitted for public use in any form or by any means, including photocopying, recording, or other electronic or mechanical methods - other than for "fair use" as brief quotations embodied in articles and reviews - without the prior written permission of the author.

The author of this book does not dispense medical advice or prescribe the use of any technique as a form of treatment for physical, emotional, or medical problems without the advice of a physician, either directly or indirectly. The intent of the author is only to offer information of a general nature to help you in your quest for emotional and spiritual well-being. In the event you use any of the information in this book for yourself, which is your constitutional right, the author and the publisher assume no responsibility for your actions.

ISBN 978-1-7361571-0-7 (paperback)
ISBN 978-1-7361571-1-4 (eBook)

Printed and bound in the United States of America

*Dedicated to all those who seek
to feel better (and better) in life*

*I so appreciate that we are
on this joyous journey together*

Contents

Introduction—My Story xi
1 The Power of this Approach—and Some Questions 1
2 Guidelines and Practicing Tips 7

Section 1—Topic Practicing

3 Streams of Good-Feeling Words 25
4 The Feelings You Want for This Topic 28
5 Positive Feelings 30
6 The Person You *Really* Are 33
7 Good-Feeling Main Statements 35
8 A Happy Journey and a Happy Ending 37
9 Simply Happy 39
10 Good-Feeling Moments 41
11 Additional (Happy) Perspectives 43
12 New Energies and New Worlds 45
13 Your Own Uplifting Words 47
14 Specific Topic: Your Body 50
15 Specific Topic: A Relationship 55
16 Specific Topic: Abundance 59
17 Specific Topic: Work 62
18 Specific Topic: Your Passions / Projects 69

Section 2—Overall-You Practicing

19 The Core Wellness Underlying All Things 75
20 The Many, Many Things in Your Favor 77
21 More and More of *the Real You* 79

22	Good-Feeling Main Statements	82
23	Better and Better Habits in Your Life	87
24	Great Feelings in Your Day	89
25	Great Things in Your Life	91
26	Better Feelings in Upcoming Days	93
27	Happy Images	94
28	Simply	99
29	Imagine	101
30	You, *Amplified*	103

Section 3—Soothing

31	Soothing Path #1: Get Some Relief When You are Upset	107
32	Soothing Path #2: Set the Topic Aside for a While	125
33	Soothing Path #3: Write Downstream Thoughts about the Topic (or) Do the Focus Wheel Process	131
34	Soothing Path #4: Identify the Feelings You *Want* for the Topic—and Then Keep Focusing There, Focusing There, Focusing There	139
35	Soothing Path #5: Practice a Soothing *Mantra* for the Topic	143
36	Soothing Path #6: Combine the Above Paths for an Extra Powerful Breakthrough	151
37	Closing Thoughts	161

Acknowledgments	*162*
Appendix A - Additional Resources	*165*
Appendix B - The Advantages of the 10-Minute Practice	*166*

This isn't just about "cheering yourself up."
This is about cheering yourself up and *elevating your life*, step by step by step.

- Abraham-Hicks

Introduction—My Story

Like many people, I've tried many things over the course of my life to become happier. And I've had success with some approaches and not so much with others.

Over time I had even accumulated a set of practicing "tools" that helped me find better feelings about things going on in my life. For instance, in the morning I might imagine having a general good feeling at the end of the day. Or when something was bothering me, I learned to write down positive aspects about the topic. Or I would say, "It will work out," "This will end up serving me," or "I've solved many problems before and I can solve this one too."

I was indeed glad to have accumulated some tools that genuinely helped. But at the same time it felt a bit random. I would apply these techniques when I happened to think of them, or when I was bothered by something. So for a while now, I've been exploring how to have a more organized and focused approach to using these tools.

One day in August 2018 I had an idea about how I might do just that. It involved just one simple process and it seemed to have real possibilities. This process would use a number of my tools.

Of the various tools I had accumulated, I had a set that was very general in nature. More to the point, these were tools that did not tend to evoke resistance (bad feelings) when I used them, even with more resistant topics in my life. They included items like:

- List some positive aspects of your current situation.

- For some area in your life, rather than trying to fix what you don't want, ask "Well, what are the feelings I *do* want here?" and then simply focus, focus, focus on only those feelings for a while.

- Imagine simply feeling good about the topic a week or a month from now.

- Picture who you really are. Now picture yourself *being* that person more in the area of the topic.

I thought, what if I were to regularly practice better feelings (using practicing tools such as the above) for a specific topic in my life? And what if I were to pick a topic that did not have a huge resistance to begin with—which would increase my chances of feeling good while practicing these feelings? And to keep it even lighter, what if my practicing was really brief, as in two minutes per day for a topic, using Abraham-Hicks's approach of "get in, feel as good as I can, get out?" It would be a quick daily "blast" of better feelings for a topic. And finally, what if I were to do this for five topics in one 10-minute session every day? These 10 minutes would be a *focused practicing of better feelings* about five topics in my life, day after day after day. I could pick topics from anywhere in my life as long as they were not my most resistant topics. A topic might be my work, a project, my body, a particular relationship, a hobby, money/abundance, my residence, a pet, the upcoming week, etc.

Introduction—My Story

I liked this idea. I liked that this approach would help me steadily grow my good feelings in five areas of my life and would do so in a light-feeling manner. I liked that this approach did not get into specifics about anything that felt "off" or "wrong" about the topics, so there would be no attempt to "wrestle" any problem area into something better. And I liked that I would be practicing with multiple topics and not be obsessing over any particular one.

So I decided to try it.

The first step was to find a timer app on my phone that I could set for 10 minutes and play some kind of beeper or gong sound every two minutes. (See the "Guidelines and Practicing Tips" chapter for timer suggestions.)

Then I had to identify five topics in my life. Since my goal in this process was to focus on okay-to-better-feeling areas, I picked five topics that—while they were far from perfect—did not have huge resistance about them.

The next step was to identify my practicing tools, and this was pretty easy since I had accumulated quite a few.

I also decided to do this 10-minute session when I felt most relaxed, which for me was just before I went to bed each night. Otherwise I did not change anything. I'm pretty busy, and I just got on with my life.

Initially I did not think much about the 10-minute sessions, other than to make sure I did the session each evening. But within a few days, I noticed that I felt better in general, and in particular I felt better in the five areas in which I had been focusing. I was surprised by how much this little bit of daily practicing started to positively infiltrate my thoughts. It was as if I was simply getting more and more "used to" better feelings in these topic areas and in general.

And this was happening by simply practicing better feelings for 10 focused minutes/day.

Over the next few weeks, I started to feel a growing sense of power and confidence. In fact, I realized that this daily practice was—dare I say—changing my life! And as I was simply focusing on the feelings I wanted (vs. trying to fix problem areas), I found that the *not*-so-good-feeling stuff was starting to fade away or simply become less important. In many cases they disappeared altogether.

This was really exciting—so much so that I was quickly inspired to keep growing and refining my set of practicing tools.

After a couple of weeks, I started to switch out some other topics into the 10-minute sessions, even including some topics that were a bit more resistant (upsetting) for me. So while I was still doing five topics, they were not always the same five topics. And since this process involved proactively choosing topics and building new good-feeling energies there, it felt as if I now had a tool to channel new positive energies in any focused direction I wanted in my life!

It was not long before I decided to write this book to describe this daily practice that has been gradually transforming my life.

Fast forward... I've now been doing this practice for 18 months. It has become a powerful part of my daily life, but the practice has evolved.

First of all, I added a section (Section 2) that focuses on how we feel *overall*. This section was, in effect, an additional "topic" to be focused on for two minutes just like the other topics. It added variety to my practicing sessions, with a special focus on helping me raise my feelings in my overall life.

Introduction—My Story

During the 18 months, of course I still had problems arise or had days where I simply felt flat-out crappy (emotionally). On the tough days, when it came time to do my 10 minutes, I did not feel like doing the normal "happy" practicing. What I *really* wanted was relief—relief that was not specifically addressed in the tools I had been using. What I really wanted was some soothing of what was bothering me. So I went through my original set of tools and identified ones that were focused on soothing troubling topics. Thus was born the "Soothing" section of the book (Section 3). The tools in this section provided a whole new set of helpful practicing items and processes that I could use (in place of the normal 10-minute practicing) on days when what I wanted more than anything else was *relief*. After this change, I found that having soothing tools immediately available, ready to help whenever something was bothering me, brought these daily sessions to a whole new level. And it fit in with the daily goal of finding better feelings, because when something is bothering us, getting relief really does help us feel better.

In the next chapter, we'll discuss the power of this approach, along with addressing some common questions.

For further information on practical tools of living, see my website, www.toolsforfeelingbetter.com.

In this book, you will see references to "Abraham" or "Abraham-Hicks." This refers to the joyful, transformative teachings of Esther and Jerry Hicks, whose work has been particularly helpful in my own journey. For more information, see www.Abraham-Hicks.com.

Terminology

Universe = The positive force that underlies our world. Feel free to substitute Source Energy, Higher Power, or God.

Inner Being = The larger, eternal part of each of us where pure joy resides. Your Inner Being is always offering you guidance in the form of emotions to let you know whether your thoughts are in alignment with your Inner Being (positive emotions) or not in alignment with your Inner Being (negative emotions). Your Inner Being also offers insights and inspiration, and the more you can relax, the better you can receive these insights and inspiration.

Law of Attraction = Like attracts like. For example, you happen to think of some off-the-wall topic and then in the next few days you run into that topic multiple times. A key recommendation in this book is to take advantage of the Law of Attraction by regularly practicing good-feeling thoughts, which then tends to bring more good-feeling thoughts, ultimately resulting in feeling better and better.

Contrast = Something you don't want. However, it does not need to cause resistance (i.e. a bad feeling). An example is seeing something on a menu you don't like and don't want—this normally does not cause a bad feeling. Another example is when you see something you want to buy and you cannot afford it. There is contrast because not being able to afford it is something you do not want. But, as in all contrast, you then have a choice as to the thoughts you then choose. In this case you could choose thoughts of frustration and disappointment, or you could choose thoughts that help you feel *energized and excited* about finding a way to create a new source of income in order to buy what you want.

Resistance = feeling bad. This occurs when you react to life's contrast with negative thoughts, which then results in bad feelings.

Alignment = To be aligned is to be in sync with one's joyful Inner Being, or, we might say, to have no internal conflicting thoughts. We always want to be as aligned as possible. You are *aligned* if you are going in a certain direction in life and are completely clear, sure, and happy about going in that direction; we might say that "all of you" (including your thoughts and feelings) are going in that one direction. Let's say you've made a decision to attend college at night. If you are clear, sure, and excited about this, you are aligned about going in this direction. But if you sign up to attend, all the while wondering whether this is the right direction for you, you have conflicting thoughts and are not fully aligned with this.

Vibration = What you are *emanating*. This is what the Law of Attraction is responding to at all times, and is therefore what determines what gets attracted into your life. For any topic, what you are vibrating is indicated by how you (truly) feel. The Universe does not respond to your words—the Universe responds to how you truly feel about a topic. That is why this book advocates practicing better feelings about topics in our lives. Not only does this feel better, this improves our vibration and therefore improves what we attract into our lives.

You create your own reality. And today we want to say that in the clearest way yet: You create the vibrational atmosphere which equals your vibrational point of attraction, and then, the Law of Attraction matches you with things like you."
   Abraham-Hicks, Phoenix, AZ on 2/1/14

1

The Power of This Approach— and Some Questions

What are the benefits of doing a daily focused practicing of better feelings? One of the biggest benefits is that it can help improve your overall "set point" or "the main feeling-level at which you live." A daily focused practicing of better feelings can be done in a variety of ways. While this book focuses on a particular 10-minute process, it can also be an activity such as quieting your mind, doing a guided meditation, or sitting quietly in your garden appreciating.

I have been doing the daily 10-minute process found in this book for many months now, and while of course I still have times when I feel "off" in my life, my "off-ness" is milder, and I tend to bounce back more easily. I really am living at higher overall feeling levels.

Of course sometimes truly awful events happen—we lose our job or become ill. If something like this occurs, and you have been doing this kind of daily practicing, you will find the practicing serves you particularly well, as it will help you more easily come back up for air. You will more easily keep perspective. You will more easily *re-find yourself*. This is because you are now more used to, or "practiced in," feeling good; the daily practice has become a solid foundation/steadying-place for you, a rock in your life.

Besides those long-term benefits, this daily habit also provides the simple joy of spending 10 minutes (every day) with good-feeling words, thoughts, and feelings. The book contains a wide variety of practicing items to choose from, along with a diversity of approaches. That can help maintain a feeling of *freshness* in your practicing, and is an exciting reminder that there are many ways to feel good/better about topics in your life. For example, chapter 6 reminds you to be "The Person You Really Are" in the area of your life where you are focusing. And chapter 9 reminds you not to overthink things and just to be "Simply Happy."

* * *

Let's look at some common questions about the 10-minute practice:

I feel really stressed in many areas of my life right now. What good does 10 minutes a day do when it all feels so overwhelming?

When you take a first step towards feeling better, initially it can seem so very small compared to the huge number of "crazy" things going on in your life. However, to begin with, the 10 minutes/day will help you feel at least a little better when you actually do it. It is like a focused "injection" of good/better feelings every single day, in comparison to *not* doing it—that is, to having the same overwhelmed feelings that you've possibly been having.

Additionally, many people have no idea how remarkably cumulative this "small" daily habit can be. As I mentioned in the introduction, after doing these practicing sessions for just one week, I noticed that not only did I feel better during each session, I also felt better overall. Over time this practice can take its place in your life as a powerful daily tool to help you keep growing and growing better feelings in your life.

This seems to be such a simple (simplistic?) approach to feeling better about topics in my life. Don't I need to 'get to the bottom' of things that are bothering me?

First of all, consider that there is no real "bottom" to the various issues in our lives—that as we focus on trying to get to the root of an issue, the Law of Attraction tends to bring us more evidence of the problem area as a result of our focus on that part of the topic.

It is remarkable that how we feel about a topic is based so much on our simple *practiced/habitual* thoughts and feelings about the topic. We tend to so easily go right to the same thoughts and feelings that we've been practicing. Sometimes these thoughts and feelings feel great. But when our thoughts about a topic are habitually focused on a problem area, then whenever we think about the topic, we think of the problem area. By continually focusing on a problem area, we are maintaining a dominating feeling of PROBLEM regarding the topic.

The 10-minute practice described in this book emphasizes *the feelings we want* for the various topics in our lives. In the *topic-practicing section* (Section 1) we skip the analyzing-of-the-problem part and instead simply focus on phrases, images, etc. that feel *good*, that are centered on growing and building the feelings we *want* for the topic rather than trying to stop the parts we don't want.

By doing this practicing of better feelings day after day, we become increasingly *accustomed to* feeling better in these areas of our lives (and overall). I have found it remarkable, even astonishing, that this simple approach can be so effective in improving how I feel about a topic, even for more difficult topics. Abraham says the results we get in our lives are all about "attraction, attraction, attraction." This practice provides a method to grow and attract the feelings we want into our lives.

So, to those who question whether this method really works, I suggest to simply try it—give it a few days or a few weeks. See if it starts to improve how you feel about individual topics, and about life in general.

What good does it do to find better feelings if my physical circumstances stay the same?

For instance...
What good does it do to find better feelings if I am still fat?
What good does it do to find better feelings if I still don't have a job?
What good does it do to find better feelings if I still don't have my lover?

In response to this, I would ask, "Where do good results in one's life originate?" From what I have seen in my own life and in others', I believe that good *results* come from good *feelings*. That is, confident, positive and happy feelings, relaxed feelings, aligned feelings. Therefore, by improving one's core feelings day by day, good results start to follow, bit by bit—it is the Law of Attraction in action. In a very real sense, *our core good feelings are the source of good-feeling results in our lives.* And, amazingly, we can shift our core feelings without needing the physical facts to change. Having said that, it has been my experience that as I have step-by-step improved my core feelings, my physical life has shifted to match my improved core feelings.

But even besides any physical manifestations, *if you truly improve your core feelings, in a real sense you change your whole world.* This is because our internal *feeling world* is in so many ways the true world in which we live. Consider—have you ever been troubled by something and then, for whatever reason, been able to find a deep feeling of "things are going to be alright?" The relief is palpable. It is like the whole world has shifted, and yet many times not a single fact has changed. And in that moment you know the power of simply improving one's core feelings about a topic.

Let's now look at one more key benefit to this approach.

There is a powerful advantage to focusing almost exclusively on where you are going, on where you want and intend to go.

Many "master creators" have demonstrated this. A "master creator" is simply someone who focuses in a single-minded manner on where they are going. People sometimes talk about the sheer force of the personality of these people. While this is often true, I believe their ability to create is based on "the clarity of their vibration." It does not take a loud or forceful personality to be a fantastic creator—it only takes a clear, single-minded focus.

As part of this, they don't focus on, or give much importance to, the problems/obstacles they find along the way. They start by imagining where they want to go, and then—very key—they do *not* follow that up with "but here are the reasons why this will not work."

An example of this is Thomas Edison, who was remarkably single-minded in his focus on inventing. When a huge section of his factory burned down, he was extraordinarily calm. He soon felt excited about what was now before him:

> *Far from being downcast, he radiated energy and excitement as he rose to the challenge of full recovery in the new year.*
> *"I am sixty-seven... I've been through a lot of things like this. It protects a man from being afflicted with ennui."*
> (From *Edison* by Edmund Morris, page 169)

Another example is Elon Musk. It was his single-minded belief and focus on his visions that brought them to life—truly new things such as financially-successful (and exciting) electric cars and reusable rocket ships—things many people said could not be built.

Our goal in this book is simpler. Our goal is not specific physical results (although physical results often happen as a result). Our goal is simply to feel as good as we can in our daily 10-minute practicing sessions. This not only feels good, but then has a remarkable cumulative effect. It positively infiltrates our thoughts and feelings in the day, and grows in our lives. It becomes a daily path in which we keep growing and growing better feelings in our lives.

In the next chapter we'll discuss the specifics of how to do the process.

Guidelines and Practicing Tips

Anything that you are wanting: don't stand in the lack of it and lament that it isn't there and expect it to come to you. It cannot. Find a little piece of it, a little trail of it, a little clue of it—look for something about it, and focus upon that little piece, and by Law of Attraction, watch it grow!

– Abraham 2/16/91

And so I started to practice the feelings I wanted. And then I practiced a bit more. And then more and more and more. I kept practicing any bits of good feelings I could find. And bit by bit this became what I felt.

The Basics of the 2 x 5 Method of Practicing Better Feelings

Below is what you need to get started. The process requires only three things:

1. A timer

Look for a timer that can be set for a total of 10 minutes, along with producing some type of signal (a beep, gong or vibration) when it reaches each two-minute mark (at two minutes, four minutes, six minutes, etc.).

For a timer on my phone, I use Timeless (iPhone only / free / www.timeless-meditation.us) or, on occasion, Seconds Pro Interval Timer (iPhone or Android / $4.99). There are a number of other apps that also work well for this.

2. Areas of your life to focus on during the 10 minutes

You will need five topics to focus on for each of the two-minute segments. You can choose any mix of topics you like, including the more general topic of "you overall." Alternatively, if something is bothering you, you can instead use the entire 10 (or more) minutes to do one of the soothing items found in Section 3.

A topic can be any subject. Here are some examples:

- Your body
- A specific relationship
- Relationships with people in general
- Money/abundance
- What you do/your job/your career
- A passion of yours (exercising, writing, acting, etc.)
- Your Vision (whatever this might mean to you)
- A project or something you are trying to create

- A skill you are working on improving
- A pet
- Your house, garden, or vehicle
- A common moment in your day or week in which you want to improve your feelings (e.g. when you wake up, when you arrive at work, when you walk into meetings, when you arrive home, sleeping, weekends, playing with your kids, etc.)
- A specific image of yourself (for example as a leader, teacher, expert, community activist, athlete, artist, friend, etc.)
- The main feelings you have and carry with you wherever you go
- Your upcoming week
- You overall

Below are some example "topic sets" for a given practicing session (10-minute period). You can see the many variations that you can use in a practicing session:

- My pet, my relationship with my sister, my house, my body, my day tomorrow (These items would all use Section 1 practicing items.)

- Me overall (This uses Section 2 practicing items for the whole 10 minutes.)

- My work, my partner, my project, me overall, me overall (This uses Section 1 practicing items except "me overall" that uses Section 2 practicing items - Note that "me overall" is repeated. You can always repeat a topic if you like.)

- Visualizing lots of happy feelings in my upcoming week for the full 10 minutes (For this topic, you can use Section 1 or Section 2 practicing items. Alternatively, this can also be completely free-form—that is, no practicing items from the book, just spontaneous visualizing.)

- "I just need some soothing today" or "I want to clean up some resistance I'm feeling about a particular area of my life" (This uses a process from Section 3.)

When you are first learning the 2 x 5 process (for the first couple of weeks or so), choose topics that are not your most resistant topics. It will be easier to feel good using these lighter topics, and this will also help you gain confidence in the process.

What if you cannot find five decent-feeling topics in your life? Then choose just one topic. Or two, three, or four. The goal here is to make it as easy as possible to feel good in your session.

Consider focusing on the same five topics every day for a while (for instance, in chunks of two to three weeks). For me, this has been powerful because it allows me to feel better, *tangibly* better, in five specific areas in my life. It is also easier to jump into my session each day since I do not have to make any decision regarding which topics to use. Of course feel free to vary this if you'd like. Do what feels best to you.

Additionally, within the 10-minute sequence, consider placing the best-feeling of the five topics as your first topic. This not only allows you to easily feel good as soon as you begin your 10 minutes, but also generates some immediate positive momentum for the whole practicing session. And note that you can improve your feelings even in your best-feeling topic!

After you've practiced for a couple of weeks or so, feel free to include topics that have a bit more resistance. If you do include a resistant topic, consider putting it toward the middle or end of the 10-minute session so that you start out with building some good-feeling momentum with easier topics before you get to the more difficult one. Try not to force it. If something really does not feel good, you can also skip that topic for today or take the 10 (or more) minutes to soothe it using one of the soothing processes found in Section 3. *Having said that, I recommend that in the long-term you do the great majority of your daily practicing using better-feeling topics (using Sections 1 and 2) as you don't want to set up a habit of continually focusing on (or "residing in") more resistant areas in your life.*

Finally, open up your mind to topics that are not listed above. What interesting or creative topics might you identify? Remember that this is a tool that allows you to channel new positive energies in any focused direction you want in your life. In what areas do you want to feel really good? Where in your life do you want to awaken better, or even *exciting,* feelings?

3. Practicing Items

The practicing items, or "practicing tools," make up the majority of this book. Which practicing items should you choose each day?

The simplest path is to just begin with the first practicing chapter (Chapter 3), and then each day continue from where you left off the day before.

Another choice is to simply turn to any chapter that appeals to you that day and start there.

Additionally, Chapter 13 presents an optional process in which you can write your own uplifting words, and provides some sample statements to get you started.

Also note that Chapters 14-18 are each dedicated to one of five specific topics:

- Your Body
- A Relationship
- Abundance
- Work
- Your Passions / Projects

When you are practicing one of these topics, consider using one of the above chapters, in addition to using the more general practicing items found in Chapters 3-13. If you find one of the specific-topic chapters to be especially powerful, consider practicing the items in that chapter multiple days in a row, just for the sheer pleasure of growing the good feelings described there. However, it is a balance. There was a time while writing the book that I was having a particular issue with my health. So I decided to do a special daily practicing session using the Chapter 14 "Your Body" phrases and words. However, after a time I realized that was exactly the *wrong* time to use these practicing items since they are more specific. *When you are feeling resistant about something in your life, go more general.* Once I realized that, I practiced using the more general items in Chapters 3-13, and that was much better.

Regarding how you read or absorb the practicing items, you can use a variety of "media":

2 - Guidelines and Practicing Tips

- Physical book
- Paper (For this method use a copier or scanner to copy and then print items from the book. You can also download and print some sample chapters from Section 2 by going to my website www.toolsforfeelingbetter.com.)
- E-Reader/Tablet/Phone
- My friend Sherry also pointed out that there is a "read aloud" option on many phones (To learn how to do this, google "read aloud phone")

It is helpful to have the practicing items (the physical book, the digital version, or the paper copies) "at the ready" when you are about to practice, as you want to make it easy to start your practicing each day.

> If you'd like a more structured approach for a topic, you can create a special practicing document just for that topic. To do that, copy or scan (and then print) the practicing chapters you'd like to use for the topic. Then use that document when you get to that topic (stepping your way through it day by day). This can be an excellent way to keep injecting new, fresh-feeling good energies into your thoughts about that topic. You can also keep a pen nearby, so that you can cross out or modify the wording of any items as it pertains to that topic. Also consider circling items that feel particularly good, and/or adding your own items.

When to Practice

With a goal of setting yourself up for success, choose a time of day when you tend to feel good. For some this might be in the morning, with the idea of starting from a place of feeling rested and fresh. For others, this might be after getting home from work before unwinding and preparing for a nice evening. Or it might be just before bedtime as you let your mind go and you prepare for a restful slumber. Consider what would most align with your schedule and your natural rhythms.

You can also vary the location: indoors, outdoors, sitting, walking. It can be pleasurable to walk and visualize, or even to walk and talk about good-feeling things out loud.

A Sample Practicing Sequence

Let's look at a sample practicing session. You start with the three required items:

- A timer
- Your list of five topics in the order in which you will be practicing them today
- The practicing items you will be using today (in hardcopy or electronic form) Let's say that you've been taking a sequential path through the practicing items. If you last practiced using Chapter 4 ("The Feelings You Want for This Topic"), today you would start with Chapter 5 ("Positive Feelings").

2 - Guidelines and Practicing Tips

Start the 10-minute timer.

Begin with Topic #1. With that topic in mind, visualize using the practicing items in the "Positive Emotions" chapter. Try to *feeeel* the feeling behind the words—and then, if some good-feeling variation or tangent occurs to you, pause and direct your focus there as well. Do the visualizing in whatever way that feels best to you.

If, after about 45 seconds (for example), you feel "done" with all the items in that chapter, move on to the next chapter ("The Person You *Really* Are") for the same topic. Let's say that feels really good and before you know it, you hear the two-minute gong/timer/vibration.

Two-Minute Mark—Change to Topic #2

You now focus on Topic #2. You could continue with the "The Person You *Really* Are" items but you decide to go to Chapter 7: "Good-Feeling Main Statements." You stay there for the full two minutes, and then hear the gong/timer/vibration at the four-minute mark.

Four-Minute Mark—Change to Topic #3

You now focus on Topic #3. You proceed to Chapter 8 ("A Happy Journey and A Happy Ending") and with Topic #3 in mind, focus on those practicing items.

You continue with this pattern until you reach the 10-minute mark. That's it! And now you move on to the rest of your day.

The rest of this chapter has some additional tips to help you in your practicing. However, if you are eager to get started, feel free to jump ahead to the practicing items. Then, at some point, consider returning here to check out these additional tips.

Also remember that you don't have to read the whole book before you begin practicing. You can keep this simple—just identify five topics and begin. Or go to the Table of Contents, find a chapter that looks appealing, and begin practicing. A couple that you might want to consider are Chapter 3 ("Streams of Good-Feeling Words") and Chapter 22 ("Good-Feeling Main Statements").

The Process of Practicing

Begin with clear intent

Begin with a clear intent to try to find the very best feelings you can find today (while setting all other things aside).

Keep listening inside as you go

As you practice, listen inside, gently guiding yourself toward any better feelings you can find. Never force your practicing down any practicing path that is not working. In other words, don't try to "push the noodle" (Abraham). In fact, if the practicing is not helping you feel better, stop altogether, try a different set of practicing items, or do a soothing process in Section 3.

Skip or cross out any items that do not help you feel better. And if focusing on an item feels particularly good, stay there longer. In fact, if you start to feel some big or exciting energies, feel free to fly off script! I usually follow the basic two minutes (x 5) setup, but sometimes I get so excited about a topic that I stay on that topic for more than the normal two minutes (including going beyond the 10-minute time frame). I also have had times when I realized it felt better to do free-form visualizing for the entire 10 minutes, so I switched over to doing that instead.

It is about feelings, not repeating words

In your practicing, you are reading (or listening to) the words of the practicing items. But remember that the real goal is to find and practice better *feelings* rather than doing rote repeating of words, so keep reaching for the better *feelings* behind the words or images. Sometimes it can help to pause for a given item, close your eyes, and then just listen inside for the better feelings. As a variation, you could even go really slow in your practicing, such as focusing on each bullet item for as long as 10-30 seconds.

Simply aim for "better"

Don't try to get more than can be easily offered.
- Abraham, 7/1/17 Seattle

When you practice, simply aim for "better" rather than trying to find some kind of perfect feeling. Sometimes these are just whiffs of better feelings. Just try to get "in the vicinity" of better feelings, and then leave the rest up to the Universe. It's much better to say "I feel a bit better—good!" rather than "This did not completely get me to my ideal state or solve the whole topic." Abraham uses the beautiful phrase "better enough."

In fact, "better" in any regard is a glorious thing. It is glorious because, first of all, it is better in those moments. "Better" is also wonderful because of the remarkable cumulative effect of little bits of "better" day after day. What starts as "slightly better feelings" can, over time, become so much more than that.

Keep it light and fresh

Do your best to keep your practicing light, fun, and playful. It also helps to keep a feeling of *freshness* in your practicing. I have included a large and varied number of practicing items in the book to help with this. (The sheer number of these tools, including tools outside this book, can remind us that there are many, many ways to feel good about topics in our lives.)

As you practice, see your improving feelings as *the Real You,* **as these good feelings are natural to who you really are**

There is real power in seeing your growing good feelings as being *central* to who you are (and the good feelings actually are). It can also help to think of these growing good feelings as more and more *unconditional*, as in "this is simply who I am." And as you increasingly BE and BEAM these powerful good feelings from deep within, by the Law of Attraction many other good feelings and circumstances come your way. Current circumstances may come and go, but it is in our most practiced (and established) good feelings where our true power lies.

Recently, I have been imagining and practicing better and better feelings in my relationship with my wife. (And I know that she has been doing her own version of practicing better feelings for our relationship.) However, a few Saturdays ago we found ourselves arguing about something in the early afternoon. Soon after, we each went our separate ways to do errands. When we got back together, it felt clear that we would quickly find our way to a resolution—*it felt like there was some strong underlying good-feeling force driving this.* And, in fact, we did come to a quick resolution. A few years ago, that would *not* have been true—the bad feelings might have lasted hours or days—but we felt the dominant power of our well-practiced good feelings.

Simple, contented devotion to a daily practice

"Find peace in the simplicity of your dedication."
- *The Portable Personal Trainer* by Eric Barr, page 31

Consider that it is easier to simply choose to do the practicing every day rather than debating with yourself whether you'll do it each day. But whatever you choose to do, do it with clear intent.

A few months ago, I came to that same realization with my evening dental care. I used to go through a nightly thought process regarding how much of my full nightly dental care to do. It finally dawned on me that it is easier and less stressful to simply do all of it every night. Now I just do it. And I do the same with my 10-minute practicing; I simply made the decision to "punch the practicing clock" every day. Some people like to use apps to help them maintain this consistency. Sample apps are Strides (iPhone) and the Fabulous app (Android).

As an alternative, consider Austin Kleon's super simple "30-Day Challenge." In this challenge, you choose *one thing* you're going to do for the next 30 days, and then each day, as you do it, you mark it off with an X on a chart. My wife and I are having great fun doing this right now, and are using Austin's excellent downloadable PDF for this: https://austinkleon.com/2017/11/01/30-day-challenge/

There are many good ways to practice using the tools in this book

There is no substitute for actual *practicing* of better feelings. However, this practicing can take many forms besides the 2 x 5 format.

When I shared this practice with friends, I quickly learned that they would use the practicing items in this book in ways that were different from the 2 x 5 format. Sometimes they would simply start reading and visualizing. My friend Rosemary sometimes reads through some of the practicing items on her breaks at work. So do the practicing in whatever way that feels best to you.

Here are some of the ways you can practice:

2 - Guidelines and Practicing Tips

- The standard 2 x 5 = 10-minute process (See Appendix B for a discussion of some advantages of this format.)
- Practicing during your daily walk (or other exercise such as on a stationary bike)
- Practicing on breaks at work
- Practicing while waiting in line, for instance at the Post Office
- Practicing in bed at night just before going to sleep
- Doing an "avalanche" of good feelings—see below

Consider a one-week (or month) "avalanche" of good feelings

How we feel in life is based on the thoughts that we currently have the most *activated*. This means that it is not based on some immovable set of "core beliefs" we have deep inside. It is simply based on our recent most-practiced thoughts. This means that if you don't like how you've been feeling lately, with regular practice you can change your "most activated" thoughts and feelings. The daily 10-minute session is one practice that can help with this.

But what if you want to take this a step further? For instance, what if you were to do 5 five-minute practicing sessions throughout the day (outside of the 2 x 5 format)? I did this kind of practicing a few years ago, and had a saying: "5 before 5." I would try to do 5 five-minute practicing sessions before 5 pm every day. (Note: When you do this, make sure not to force yourself to practice when you are feeling lousy—that will just backfire!) For me, doing the "5 before 5" really helped me boost my overall feelings since I simply had my thoughts more often in these better-feeling places.

This plan to "go for it" can be lots of fun. If this appeals to you, try it out—consider doing this (or some variation) for a week, a month, or whatever time frame feels good. Take a look at your schedule and see what kind of "avalanche schedule" is realistic for you. Then set a clear intention. You might also keep a chart (including "make-up" practicing sessions if you miss one). Keep the stakes low and keep the whole thing fun. With the right spirit, this can be a fantastic, and even transformative, approach.

No matter your approach, keep (gently) aiming for higher and higher feeling levels

As I have continued to do this practicing, I have realized that I can coast along and practice some of the same things over and over. That is indeed beneficial as it keeps my vibration, my main-feeling place, at a good level. But, when I aim for *new* good-feeling places and new *levels* of good feelings, then it can get really exciting. As you practice, day by day, consider looking for, aiming for:

- ever deeper good feelings
- more solidity in your good feelings
- deeper happiness
- new levels of fun
- new levels of excitement
- new levels of joy

Now, on to the practicing items!

Section 1 - Topic Practicing

Streams of Good-Feeling Words

"And in that moment, I felt some new,
wonderful feelings open up."

Focus on your topic and then, as you read each item below, find the feeling as best you can.

- simple joy

- good energy in the air

- new happy thoughts

- bright colors all around this topic

- more and more of a *lightness* here

- more and more of *an easy feeling* here

- more and more *happiness* here

- deeper and deeper wellness

- so many good things

- a comfortable journey

- a happy journey

- enjoying myself more and more

- more and more moments of *playing*

- a free and easy and hearty laugh

- feelings of *magical*

- finding some great next steps

- solutions popping up

- more and more solutions

- feeling exciting progress

- a deep joy at the center of it all that keeps growing

- feeling my alignment improving

- feeling more solid and secure

- a deep, growing *confidence*

3 - Streams of Good-Feeling Words

- strong and clear and confident

- feeling like *myself* more and more

- finding whole new levels of good feelings

- new sparks and new happy energies

- new great ideas

- things opening up in exciting ways

- my world growing bigger and bigger in this area of my life

- Oh, what an exciting spirit of life I'm feeling here!

- Life is good.

4

The Feelings You Want for This Topic

*"And in that moment, I focused on the feelings
I wanted, and I began to feel them more and more."*

There is a significant benefit in identifying the feelings you *want* for a topic. When you identify these feelings, you then have "organizing points" or "organizing planets" around which you can then focus your practicing, resulting in better and better feelings in areas that matter most to you.

In this chapter, identify the feelings you *want* for your topic. (You can also ask, "What is the 'feeling-essence' of what I want for this topic?")

For example, here are some feelings you might identify for your work:

- in balance
- centered
- satisfying work
- a feeling that I contribute
- lots of fun
- a feeling of playing
- really happy here

4 - The Feelings You Want for This Topic

- engaged
- good flow in my days
- thriving
- an overall good feeling

In doing your own list, you might list fewer feelings, or many more.

Often we want a feeling that is the *opposite* of some negative feeling we are currently experiencing. In these cases, make sure to choose a phrase that is positive since the positive phrase will do less invoking of your current negative feelings. For instance, instead of saying that you want your partner to treat you better, you might say "an overall good feeling in this relationship." Or instead of talking about pain in your body going away, you might say "a happy-feeling body."

After you've completed your list, read back through it and try to *feel* each feeling, one at a time. It's ok if at this point you can only find a whiff of the feeling—just do the best you can from where you are right now.

Consider identifying the feelings you want for *each* main topic in your life. If you do this, and then regularly practice the feelings, your life will start to shift in the direction of these more practiced feelings. *Your life is always shifting in the direction of your most practiced/habitual feelings.*

5

Positive Feelings

"And in that moment, I felt so many wonderful things."

Practicing the feelings of *positive emotion* words and phrases can be a simple way to practice better feelings about a topic. And because this is a general focus, it also tends to be less resistant. Below are some of these words and phrases. Focus on your topic and then, as you read each item below, find the feeling as best you can.

- lightness

- ease

- easy

- letting go

- having fun

- satisfying

- interesting, fascinating, *inspiring*

- *playing* with it
- new energy, *fresh energy*
- a light and fun trying out of new things
- learning and expanding
- eager and excited
- comfortable flow, happy flow, joyous flow
- feeling at home
- friendly, neighborly
- love
- relaxed and open
- joyful
- things working out well
- feeling the core wellness
- things improving
- simply happy

Section 1 - Topic Practicing

- feeling like the Real Me here

- in balance

- solid, stable, sure

- moving with clarity and decisiveness

- confident

- new levels of happy feelings

- sensing, intuitive

- exciting

- *magical*

- a feeling of "I can do this / we can do this"

- a powerful thriving

- exciting worlds opening up

- more and more *mastery*

- happy ending

The Person You *Really* Are

*"And in that moment, I felt the fullness of myself...
I felt myself being the person I really am."*

Consider for a moment who you really are. And now picture yourself *being* that person more and more in the area of this topic.

Now extend that into feeling the following characteristics:

My Growing Knowing of the Wellness
- "It's working out well"
- deeply centered
- more and more comfortable and relaxed in this topic
- an overall good feeling about this topic
- exuding joy

My Choosing/Initiating/Leading
- led and powered from within
- a clear chooser, initiator, leader
- competent, clear, on top of things, ahead of things
- a clear, strong, aligned approach in this area of my life
- my natural stability, sureness, strength

- a confident and expanding *being*
- a bigger and bigger sense of myself

My Play, My Fun
- my natural playfulness
- more and more fun here
- excitedly trying out new things
- more and more *thrilled*

My Expanding / Thriving
- normal, natural, *easy* thriving
- easily being in a thriving mode, like a needle resting in the groove of a vinyl record
- my "thriving mode" growing and growing and growing
- even having (more and more) feelings of *mastery*

Good-Feeling Main Statements

"And in that moment, I felt the core wellness within this topic, and felt a growing confidence."

Imagine each of the following statements and trends in the area of the topic.

- So many things about this topic are good.

- I am doing so many things right.

- Things are improving.

- I am making great progress.

- I am on track. *I am on track.*

- I can do this. (More and more I *am* doing this.)

- I can thrive here. (More and more I *am* thriving here.)

- My overall sense of wellness here is growing.

- I'm feeling more and more aligned in my path.

- My feelings of *knowing* are growing.

- I am feeling more and more like *the Real Me*.

- I am feeling happier and happier.

- My core of joy in this topic is growing and growing.

- More and more, I'm getting *used to* feeling really good in this area of my life.

- Things are good. Life is good.

8

A Happy Journey and a Happy Ending

"And in that moment, I felt real ease about my upcoming path, and felt a new sense of fun and adventure opening up."

As we think about what we want for a topic in our lives, we often focus on the result. But what do we imagine for the journey? Sometimes, even when we are imagining a happy ending, in the back of our minds we are thinking this will be a difficult journey. And in doing that, we are pre-paving (practicing the feeling of) a difficult journey. If we instead imagine *good* feelings about the journey, we can experience a much better-feeling journey. The journey is indeed where we live, and there is such satisfaction, learning, fun, adventure, excitement, and joy available to us in our journeys.

- Imagine feeling relaxed and happy in your journey in this area of your life.

- See yourself more and more *simply in a good mood* in your journey with this topic.

- Imagine some happy words:
  "I'm having such fun along the way. In fact, it feels like I'm *playing* with the Universe in this unfolding."
  "The Universe often surprises and delights me here."
  "Wow, things are turning out so well."

- Imagine taking your journey with a feeling of *solutions, solutions, solutions*.

- Imagine easy resolutions of glitches along the way.

- Imagine lots of happy endings along the way.

- Picture yourself simply having a great-feeling day tomorrow in the area of this topic.

- Imagine whole new levels of good-feelings about this topic a week or a month from now.

- Imagine yourself at some point in the future *realizing how incredibly good this whole topic has been for you.* As you look back, you feel so appreciative about the whole journey, and how the contrast/challenges were so worth it, as they helped you find great joy in this area of your life.

Simply Happy

> "And in that moment, I decided that my goal is to be simply happy... simply happy in my life, and simply happy in the area of this topic."

- Practice feeling "the happy spirit" of this topic.

- Imagine feeling more and more *relaxed* about the topic.

- Imagine things getting easier and easier in the area of the topic.

- Visualize how you are truly finding your way in the area of the topic.

- Imagine feeling lighter and lighter about the whole topic.

- Feel yourself as more and more of a cooperative component with your Inner Being in focusing on the good-feeling aspects of this topic.

- Imagine more and more moments of true, relaxed *playing* in this area of your life.

- Imagine trying things out, and having lots of fun adventures.

- Picture *sparks* of good energy around the topic.

- Practice the feeling of *magical* in the area of the topic.

- Practice the feeling of "simply happy."

10

Good-Feeling Moments

"And in that moment, I felt something new...
something that felt very, very exciting."

Think of the topic, and then imagine the *feeeeling* of each of these moments:

- "I'm making progress, and I can feel things getting easier, bit by bit by bit."

- "I just felt an exciting *lightness* about this topic."

- "Just now I thought about the topic and realized how good it now feels."

- "Ooohhh, I found a great next step."

- "Ooohhh, I'm feeling my growing alignment here."

- "I *like* this idea!"

- "Wow—*that* felt inspired."

Section 1 - Topic Practicing

- "I feel like I'm just a kid playing and playing and playing."

- "I just felt some wonderful new feelings."

- "And right then I realized I was happy... just really, really happy."

- "I am feeling really good."

11

Additional (Happy) Perspectives

*"And in that moment, I found a whole new way
to see and feel the joy in this topic."*

The practicing items in this chapter provide new (happy) perspectives about the topic. Take your time as you consider each one:

- Quiet your mind for a moment. Then lightly think of the topic... letting it breathe... Then listen quietly for anything your Inner Being (your inner guidance) might be telling you about this topic.

- Do you know that what you want already exists *vibrationally*? (per Abraham) All you need to do is relax a bit more... and feel everything is on track a bit more... to feel more of your vibrational creation. This is indeed the path... to day by day keep finding any little bits of these better feelings that you can.

- Imagine what it would be like to be exactly where you want to be in the area of this topic. *Feel* this way of being... these feelings... as if they are true right now.

- Answer the question: "What is it about what I want for this topic... that is so lovely... that feels so good?"

- Imagine being born anew, in this very day.
  Born anew! And you can choose anything you want. What feelings would you choose in this area of your life from this day forward?

- Visualize yourself as a young person who is excited and *ready to go for it* in life. And as you think about the topic, feel your confidence and excitement about what lies ahead.

- Imagine what it would be like to thrive at extraordinary levels in the area of this topic. Practice feeling some of this thriving right now.

- Imagine the clear and aligned feelings of those who are "masters" in this area of life. *You can tap into and feel more of that wisdom right now.* Practice feeling some of these masterful feelings.

12

New Energies and New Worlds

> "And in that moment, I felt something open up, and felt so excited."

Think of the topic, and then practice the feeling of each of the items below:

- new possibilities opening up

- new happy feelings opening up

- exciting new energies opening up

- exciting new *worlds* opening up

- excited about life... excited about the future... excited about this topic

- Imagine having a new happy thought about the topic.

- Imagine finding a great next step for the topic.

- Imagine a few specific *peak experiences* you might have in the area of the topic.

- Imagine that there are no limits as to how good this topic can get.

- Do free-form visualization. In this practicing item, just "stare off into space" and let your imagination go, imagining all kinds of good feelings and moments in the area of the topic.

13

Your Own Uplifting Words

"And in that moment, I found words that resonated within me, and it felt so good."

Consider taking a few minutes outside your normal 10-minute sessions to create your own uplifting statements. These statements can then be added to your practicing sessions.

You have your own unique perspective. Words that speak right to where you are, and uplift you, are extra powerful. What specific words might provide this personal connection for you? In this chapter, you will write your own statements to uplift your feelings about a topic.

The statements do not need to be perfect; they just need to feel better in any regard. If writing your own statements does not appeal to you, you can use some of the sample statements below, or just skip this chapter.

If you do choose to write statements, and then at some point if you find yourself writing words that feel like too much of a jump from your current beliefs, consider adding softening words such as "more and more" or "step by step." You'll see examples of this below.

Let's look at a couple of different types of statements you might write.

Section 1 - Topic Practicing

You might write *words that represent trends you want to grow*, such as:

- I'm having more and more fun in this area of my life.
- I'm feeling happier and happier here.
- More and more, I keep things light here.
- I'm feeling more and more relaxed here.
- I'm growing in my confidence here.
- I'm growing in the confidence I have in others.
- I'm getting better and better at this.
- More and more I realize I am easily and naturally healthy. (your body)
- I'm finding more and more things that I like about my work. (your work)
- I feel this whole area of my life opening up more and more. (money/abundance)
- Step by step, I'm feeling better and better about this relationship. (a relationship)

You might write *words that help you shift current negative thoughts and/or open up assumptions*, such as:

- There are a lot of good things going on here.
- I am on track.
- I am on a good path.
- It will work out.
- It can be easy.
- What I'm trying to do here is a small and easy change.

13 - Your Own Uplifting Words

- I can put what I want into place pretty easily. (for a project)
- The current stuff going on is really not that big a deal.
- There IS a solution.
- There is a path for me.
- There is a *good* path for me.
- My real goal here is joy, and there are many paths to joy.
- I can do this.
- I can thrive here.
- I can step by step find better and better feelings here.
- I can find good feelings here without needing the facts to change.
- Since the results I receive are based on "attraction, attraction, attraction" (Abraham), I'm just going to keep practicing the feelings I *want* here.
- Step by step, I am becoming a better and better spouse/parent/child/friend. (how you see yourself)
- This can be a fun journey.
- It will be fun to try a bunch of different things and see which ones work best for me.
- This could be a fun adventure.
- I'm looking forward to seeing the fun ways this will unfold.

As you practice your custom words, continue to monitor how they feel. If they feel "off" in any regard, remove or modify them. Keep fine-tuning the words in the direction of "better."

Specific Topic: Your Body

> "And in that moment, I felt some
> exciting new feelings about my body."

This is one of five chapters focused on a specific topic. This chapter is about your body. If the more specific-oriented items in this chapter evoke resistance in you, then consider setting this chapter aside (for now) and practicing using the more general items in Chapters 3-13. (When a topic is one of your more difficult topics, that is the time to go more *general* in your practicing about the topic.)

Practice the *feeling* of each of these:

- So much about my body feels good.
- growing happy feelings in my body
- happy and healthy and strong

- More and more, the cells in my body are working beautifully together.
- More and more, the cells in my body are in joyful, harmonious balance.
- My cells are feeling happier and happier.
- My body is my friend.

14 - Specific Topic: Your Body

- happy energy flowing through my body
- joy flowing through my body
- cells so happy I can feel them *dancing*
- such happy cells
- such a happy body

- a light, clear, and well-functioning body
- feeling core wellness in my body
- so much wellness in my body
  so much wellness in my body
  so much wellness in my body

- feeling so relaxed in my body
- feeling so at home in my body
- feeling so *right* in my body

- a lightness to my step
- the light and easy feeling of a five-year-old
- feeling free in my body, like a kid playing in the yard

- jumping out of bed in the morning
- excited about life
- lots of energy
- bounding up the stairs
- big energy, exciting energy
- More and more my body feels excitingly good.

- fit and trim
- light and nimble

Section 1 - Topic Practicing

- a strong torso
- a graceful, beautiful athlete

- more and more loving what I eat and drink
- The things I eat and drink are working well in my body.
- I love being really hungry and then satisfying my hunger.
- hungry and happy, hungry and happy, hungry and happy
- enjoying my food more and more
- enjoying what I drink more and more

- my body resting well at night
- finding such comfortable positions in bed
- having happier and happier thoughts at night

- moving like a joyfully healthy person moves
- moving with fluidity and grace
- lightness and ease
- enjoying my exercise, sports, and dance
- easy, joyous, almost flying movement
- exciting and fun ways to move my body
- running swiftly and lightly and easily
- feeling so light in my body
- I love moving my body.

- feeling a growing joyful sensuality and sexuality
- getting in better and better shape
- moving towards being in the best shape of my life
- I love shaping and improving my body.

- having great-looking clothes
- looking better and better
- feeling my own beauty more and more

- expanding capacities in my body
- my body functioning better and better and better
- the joy of my body becoming its real self

- My body is a "tree trunk" of great health and solidity.
- sureness in my body
- strong in my body, strong in my spirit
- happy, strong, and confident in my body
- feeling more and more invincible in my body
- faster, higher, stronger (Olympic motto)

- feeling like I'm 18, and my body and my life are growing and expanding
- so easily healthy, like an 18-year-old

- My whole body is coming into a clearing.
- Things are getting better and better.
- Great health is natural for me.
- Great health in my body feels more and more *inevitable*.
- such *vitality* in my body
- more and more moments of feeling super healthy
- my more and more *powerful* good health
- There is great health in my body.

- more and more resilient and bounce-back-able
- My body is a superstar in its abilities to adjust and to thrive.

- finding new happy feelings in my body
- more and more joy in my body
- opening myself to the wow! that is possible here

15

Specific Topic: A Relationship

*"And in that moment, I felt so comfortable
and happy about the relationship."*

This is one of five chapters focused on a specific topic. This chapter is about your relationship with a particular person. If the more specific-oriented items in this chapter evoke resistance in you, then consider setting this chapter aside (for now) and practicing using the more general items in Chapters 3-13. (When a topic is one of your more difficult topics, that is the time to go more *general* in your practicing about the topic.)

Think of your relationship, and then practice the *feeling* of each of these:

- bit by bit, feeling better and better here
- finding my way in this relationship more and more
- each on our own journey, each of our journeys to be celebrated

- going into this relationship *centered* by a joyful connection with myself
- more and more feeling like the Real Me wherever I am, including in this relationship
- a stronger and stronger sense of myself
- my own clear and powerful connection

- more and more choosing to see and be with the *Inner Being* of this person
- my Inner Being with their Inner Being
- so often seeing such wonderful things in this person
- so often projecting love and joy to this person
- so often just loving this person

- many things in common
- valuing each other's talents
- each of us being joyously ourselves
- independent, while also having great co-creating
- learning things from each other
- more and more comfortable together
- moving towards being great friends
- a connection of more and more joy
- We make a great team.

- practicing simple better feelings in this relationship
- a light feeling
- relaxed, comfortable, at ease
- more and more in balance
- not needing me to be perfect

- not needing them to be perfect
- feeling easy about the whole thing
- not giving much importance to glitches along the way
- easily resolving glitches
- fussing less and less

- letting things unfold in an easy manner
- really enjoying the moments
- interesting, satisfying, fun
- an ever-improving *flow* when we are together
- feeling open, free, relaxed
- a happy feeling in the air
- happier and happier energy

- letting fun lead the way
- laughing and good times
- laughing and laughing and laughing
- so many great things to talk about
- lots of fun and interesting conversations
- more and more fun when we are together
- so much fun together

- often feeling connected
- feeling a deeper and deeper connection
- such joy together

- having more and more *confidence* in the other person
- more and more letting go

- joyously letting them vibrate and attract for themselves
- more and more watching with admiration

- more and more feeling strong and sure in this relationship
- feeling a deep wellness here

- I am a good partner/child/parent/friend to them.
- There is so much about this person that feels good to me.

16

Specific Topic: Abundance

> "And in that moment, I felt a growing abundance all throughout my life."

This is one of five chapters focused on a specific topic. This chapter is about abundance all throughout your life (including money). If the more specific-oriented items in this chapter evoke resistance in you, then consider setting this chapter aside (for now) and practicing using the more general items in Chapters 3-13. (When a topic is one of your more difficult topics, that is the time to go more *general* in your practicing about the topic.)

Think of the general feeling of abundance, and then practice the *feeling* of each of these:

- a growing abundance in my life
- an abundance of choices
- an abundance of happy thoughts
- an abundance of fun activities
- an abundance of good ideas
- an abundance of good tv shows
- more and more areas of my life *feeling* abundant
- such plenty in my life

- feeling more and more ease and easy
- feeling light and relaxed
- a growing flow of joyous energy
- more and more feeling a wellness underneath
- more and more *knowing* the underlying wellness

- I am growing ever more and more comfortable with dollars.
- I am increasingly good with dollars.
- an easy flow
- a happy flow
- more and more sources of money opening up
- a joyous flow of dollars in my life

- so lightly and joyfully listening to my Inner Being in my journey
- more and more *in balance*
- aligned and clear
- more and more solid and sure
- a growing thriving
- a growing confidence
- more and more *knowing*

- growing choices in my life
- growing freedom in my life

- *sparks* of new and expanding energy
- expanding new ideas
- experiencing fun and exciting *examples* of abundance
- fun and easy expansion in many directions

- growing and growing the *feelings* of the things I want
- the garden I want, the house, the vehicle
- flying first class
- so many things I love all around me
- abundance all around
- more and more it is just here in my life

- fun initiating and exploring
- such fun in the unfolding!
- To the Universe: "I want to play."
- "Ooooh... what fun thing shall we do now?"

- wow... more and more exciting
- opening myself up to growing possibilities here
- feeling more and more unlimited in all areas of my life

Specific Topic: Work

"And in that moment, I felt a new level of thriving and confidence about my work."

This is one of five chapters focused on a specific topic. This chapter is about your work/job. If the more specific-oriented items in this chapter evoke resistance in you, then consider setting this chapter aside (for now) and practicing using the more general items in Chapters 3-13. (When a topic is one of your more difficult topics, that is the time to go more *general* in your practicing about the topic.)

Think about your work/job, and then practice the *feeling* of each of these:

- seeing some good things at work
- doing some really good work
- moments of real *alignment*
- moments of being in the flow
- relaxing more
- having more fun
- There are many things that feel good here.
- I'm finding better and better feelings at work.

- **CENTERED AND ALIGNED**
- more and more *choosing* my energy as I begin each day
- creator, leader, initiator
- having my own internal clear and joyful stance at work
- making sure to stay in charge of myself
- clear for myself / unapologetic
- choosing to be more myself (the Real Me) at work
- growing confidence
- strong, stable, sure
- centered and in balance
- growing excellence in what I do
- a growing, deep sense of wellness
- a strong and calming influence
- a growing, exciting clarity and decisiveness
- growing feelings of my own power, wherever I am
- exuding outwards more and more

- **MY VISION**
- completely following my Vision for myself at work
- the leader of myself there, choosing my path
- more and more aligned with myself
- going into the day with clarity, focus, and alignment
- staying focused and on track
- moving quickly, easily, and joyfully all day long

- **HAPPIER AND HAPPIER AT WORK**
- loving more and more things at my work
- finding it easier and easier to feel good
- a growing lightness in my feelings

- feeling like skipping on my way to work
- at lunch and filled with joy
- feeling better and better as the day goes on
- I am driving home from work and feeling great.
- often feeling like I am on a *Happiness Expressway*

- GREAT FLOW IN THE DAY
- a happy and clear focus throughout the day
- making sure to listen inside and be guided as I go
- focusing on one thing at a time in my segments
- feeling so happily *present* in my segments
- more and more fun and even *intoxicating* segments
- engaged, active, exciting
- happy moment after happy moment
- so often getting into a powerful Happiness Zone
- great *flow* in my days
- time flying by

- FUN
- having more and more *fun* at work
- often feeling like a fun adventure
- more and more of a fantastic playground for me
- more and more having a feeling of *playing* at work
- a growing mastery
- feeling so much mastery it is fun
- it is fun to make things better for people.
- it is so much fun to master areas at work.
- creating, playing, having fun
- so satisfying, so fulfilling

17 - Specific Topic: Work

- **EXCITED**
- eager to get to work
- I'm walking in the front door and feeling excited.
- We're doing something really exciting here.
- many great projects
- a growing underlying excitement
- I'm doing some great things here.
- We're going to do great things today.
- I'm about to begin an activity at work, and I feel very excited and very eager.
- racing back to my desk because I am so excited about something
- feelings of *magical*

- **CAMARADERIE**
- a growing, fun camaraderie
- feeling such joy with others
- lots of *playing* with others
- such laughter and silliness together
- sharing our joy with each other
- our Inner Beings cavorting
- a team that is jelling more and more
- more and more of a kick ass team
- feeling clear, ongoing, forward movement in our work
- exciting, ongoing progress in our work
- building great things together
- "We're going to get there."
- "We're getting there."

- **SKILLED AND CONTRIBUTING**
- getting better and better at what I do
- contributing more and more
- making things better and better
- skillful, competent
- on top of relevant details
- clear and on point at work
- well-organized
- eloquent
- sharp in my thinking
- at the top of my game
- getting stuff done quickly and easily
- more and more on top of things
- more and more prepared ahead of time
- moving toward exciting excellence
- so easy it's fun
- doing beautiful work
- patient, joyful craftsmanship
- many excellent ideas
- insight after insight
- growing and growing my capabilities
- prolific
- better and better approaches
- the others will have to chase after me
- creating a wake behind me
- more and more an approach of "There IS a solution"
- more and more vibrating with the whole *feeling* of solutions
- more and more "I can do it"
- more and more "I can thrive here"

- ... and "we can do it"
- ... and "we can thrive here"
- tremendous contributions at work

- **MY JOYFUL, LOVELY WAY OF BEING AT WORK**
- my easy, natural way at work
- calm and welcoming
- easily connecting with others
- I have great, happy energy.
- a core joy that just keeps growing and growing and growing
- in love with life
- relaxed and open
- feeling such ease
- feeling a joyous lightness about it all
- joyfully letting things unfold
- happily turning it all over to the Universe

- **GREAT PROJECTS, GREAT TOOLS**
- having useful and even fun tools
- More and more, my computer works so well for me.
- better and better processes

- **FLEXIBLE, ADAPTABLE**
- truly fine with change
- *thriving* with change
- powerfully and remarkably adaptable
- using the power and fresh clarity of new contrast
- feeling a core lightness about the overall flow

- THRIVING
- such growing thriving
- such *exciting* thriving
- excitedly creating and expanding
- feeling great at the end of the week

- LIFE IS GOOD
- in a joyous, right-feeling place
- more and more feeling free to be myself
- free to express and create
- more and more *being and becoming myself* at work

18

Specific Topic: Your Passions / Projects

"And in that moment, I felt whole new levels of joy and excitement about the project."

This is one of five chapters focused on a specific topic. This chapter is about a passion of yours or a project in your life. If the more specific-oriented items in this chapter evoke resistance in you, then consider setting this chapter aside (for now) and practicing using the more general items in Chapters 3-13. (When a topic is one of your more difficult topics, that is the time to go more *general* in your practicing about the topic.)

Think of your passion or project, and then practice the *feeling* of each of these:

- many, many great aspects to this project
- growing good feelings in this project
- an overall good feeling here

- more and more ease
- a growing lightness about it

- in more and more places of this journey...
  playing and playing and playing
- trying stuff out
- having more and more fun
- more and more giving priority to keeping *my happy-and-having-fun internal engine* in its central place for this project

- feeling more and more interested, and even fascinated
- discovery and adventure and newness

- what great work I'm doing
- so satisfying

- solid and sure
- more and more bringing a confidence, and a knowing, to this project
- a deeper and deeper sense of wellness

- so following my own vision
- often feeling *inspired*
- my own clearer and clearer energy
- more and more aligned and in balance
- more and more confident
- I can do it.
- I can thrive here.
- more and more on top of things
- more and more *ahead* of things
- it is getting easier and easier

- even moving into *"so easy it's fun"*
- There are no limits to how fun this journey can be.

- happier and happier
- a happy spirit in the air
- a growing joy about this project

- eager and excited about this project
- As I look forward to my next steps, I can't wait to get started.
- "I am filled with the feelings of a great project."

- clearer and clearer
- remarkable insights
- the feeling of *more and more and more solutions*

- better and better daily flow in my project
- so often *in the flow* in my segments
- more and more happily focused on whatever I am doing
- sometimes even having intoxicating, transcendent moments
- moments outside of time

- an ongoing movement forward
- more and more feelings of tangible progress
- I'm getting there.
- We're getting there.
- more and more things falling into place
- a growing feeling of success-in-progress

- joyful camaraderie
- great teamwork
- more and more feelings of connection

- patient, beautiful craftsmanship
- doing beautiful, beautiful work
- creating something really good, really exciting here
- "The recipients of this work will love it."

- many fantastic things are growing here
- going way beyond what is often done
- There are no limits as to how good the result can be.

Section 2 - Overall-You Practicing

19

The Core Wellness Underlying All Things

"And in that moment, I felt the wellness underlying all things."

Practicing the feeling of core wellness can be helpful at a fundamental level. As you find more feelings of core wellness, you get more *used to* feeling core wellness. In doing this practicing, you learn that there is no need to somehow prove wellness—you just need to practice (and practice) the *feeling* of wellness.

- Feel the wellness underlying this day.
  (There is a lot of wellness in this day.)

- Feel how you have experienced wellness in many, many ways over the course of your life.

- Imagine more and more deep good feelings growing in your life.

- Close your eyes and feel the deep wellness underlying this earth.

- "And I looked around, and felt the wellness, and the joy, of all that was around me."

20

The Many, Many Things in Your Favor

> "And in that moment, I felt many helpful forces
> all around me, working on my behalf."

There are many, many things in your favor in life. Here are a few:

1. The main force in this Universe is one of towering well-being.

2. There is a huge core tendency inside each of us to feel good.

3. "My Inner Being—the huge, purely positive part of me—is always with me, encouraging me and giving me clues for next steps."

4. "I have some wonderful tools that help me feel better."

5. "I've resolved many, many things in my life—I have shown myself time and again I have the ability to resolve issues that come my way."

- See your practicing of better feelings (and any other practices you do) as more and more powerful and helpful forces in your life.

- See your growing happiness as a more and more *powerful* happiness.

21

More and More of *the Real You*

> "And in that moment, I felt myself *being* who
> I really am, and was filled with great joy."

There is this person deep inside who is the Real You. And, as you've known for a long time, this person is capable of things that go far beyond what others have seen.

Feeling like the person you really are is so foundational to happiness that regularly practicing this feeling can transform your life. You can set aside time to do this practicing, as we do in the 10-minute practicing. It can also be done as you move about in your daily activities, such as in interactions with family, or in being a happy person on your commute, or in being your clear, confident, and thriving self at work.

In practicing this main vibe of who you really are, you will attract events and experiences based on this vibe. The Universe says, "Oh, *this* is who you are. We'll give you more of that." This is because the Law of Attraction is always giving you more of whatever matches your most activated feelings.

Below are some items to help you practice the feelings of the Real You.

- Go inside yourself for a moment. What are the feelings of *the Real You*, this person you really are? Take a moment to identify and feel the feelings of this magnificent person inside you.

- See yourself bringing more and more of the full you, the Real You, to your everyday activities.

- We should—every one of us—have our own internal swagger. This is about core confidence. Who is the *You with a Swagger?* See yourself moving with a growing confidence and swagger in your daily life.

- Practice feeling a bigger and bigger sense of yourself, wherever you are. "Many things happen around me. No matter. I am strong and clear, and I follow my own Vision."

- See yourself as more and more *the true leader of your life*. "Others do not need to change. Instead, I choose to be the leader of my life, and only focus there, while allowing others the freedom to lead themselves."

- See yourself as clear, decisive, and thriving. See yourself growing more and more confident in all you do. See yourself with a growing *mojo*.

- Imagine a powerful *moving forward* in your life.

- See yourself living a BIG life (that is, a big life to *you*).

- Consider that there are no limits to all that you can be and do and have in the world.

- See yourself as more and more being
the person you really are.

- Consider that you can grow more and more "Places of Power/Powerbases" in your life. Any location, activity, or topic that easily feels good can be a Powerbase. Some examples: mornings, evenings, Saturdays, doing yoga, gardening, sleeping, where you live, doing your 10-minute practicing sessions, etc. With practice, you can grow the powerful feeling-place of each of these. Visualize and feel the growing power of each of these "Places of Power/Powerbases" in your life.

Good-Feeling Main Statements

*"And in that moment, I realized how on track
I really am, and I felt a strong, growing confidence."*

As you read each item below, pause for a moment to find its feeling.

- So much is right in my life.

- So much is good in my life.

- I am doing really well.

- I have made huge progress.

- I am on track in my life.

- *I am on track.*

22 - Good-Feeling Main Statements

- What gifts I've been given in my lifetime!

- Things are getting better and better.

- I'm feeling lighter and lighter in my life.

- I'm becoming happier and happier.

- Life is good.

- There are big, powerful forces at work on my behalf.

- I am in a hugely advantageous position.

- I have fantastic ongoing *options* in my life.

- I have fantastic ongoing *opportunities* in my life.

- Life is in my favor.

- I easily feel good, more and more.

- I am becoming happier and happier at a core level.

- There is a huge core wellness underlying my whole being.

- My ultimate wellness is a certainty.

- And I'm having more and more fun in my life.
- I'm connecting with people more and more.
- I have more and more energy in my days.
- I feel my growing alignment in life.
- I feel my growing power in life.
- I'm thriving more and more.
- This is simply who I am.

- I am finding my path more and more, day by day.
- I am strong and clear.
- I am *robust*.
- I am finding my own clear, strong voice.

- There is a powerful, joyful energy at my core.
- This powerful joy inside me is getting bigger and bigger.
- More and more, joy fills my days and my life.

22 - Good-Feeling Main Statements

- I spread my joy wherever I go.

- I am a leader in joy.

- Things are really starting to come together for me.

- I keep improving my overall approach to life.

- I am more and more clearly guided from within.

- I make more clear decisions.

- More and more, I stay in charge in each area of my life.

- More and more, I approach things from a position of power.

- More and more, I keep things moving forward in my life.

- I fuss less and less about things that are happening around me.

- And I worry less about glitches along the way.

- There is a huge and growing positive momentum in my life.

- I am developing a clearer and clearer Vision in my life.

- Step by step, my Vision is dominating my life more and more.

- More and more, I look out into the world feeling like the Real Me, in charge, with clarity and intention, and am filled with happiness and joy.

- I feel a growing *thriving* in my life.

- I am getting stronger and stronger, and clearer and clearer.

- My capabilities keep expanding.

- My powers keep expanding.

- My mojo is growing bigger and bigger, and stronger and stronger.

- *I am the leader of my life.*

- There is so much to be excited about.

- In more and more ways, life is easy and life is fun.

- I am moving forward in so many exciting ways in my life.

- I feel my whole world expanding.

- *I am becoming myself.*

23

Better and Better Habits in Your Life

"And in that moment, I could feel the power of the habits that I had been building and building and building."

- Visualize yourself directing all your energies more and more in only one direction—towards the feelings you *want*.

- Visualize yourself heading into your days with a clear priority to look for the very best-feeling thoughts you can find, all throughout the day.

- Visualize yourself listening openly inside, sensing the nudge of your Inner Being towards helpful next steps, and towards better and better feeling thoughts.

- Visualize yourself being fully present in your current activities in the day, immersed and happy.

- Visualize yourself being more and more aware of your current energy, so that you can redirect your thoughts if the current energy does not feel good.

- Visualize yourself feeling more and more comfortable with any contrast that comes your way, and even powerfully (and excitedly) *using* the energy of the contrast.

- Visualize yourself approaching more and more things in your life from a standpoint of "I can do it," "I can thrive here," and "I can have fun here."

24

Great Feelings in Your Day

"And in that moment, I felt a great and happy spirit in myself, and in this day."

- See yourself in the day looking around from where you are, and savoring and loving and adoring and appreciating so many wonderful things.

- Imagine *transcendent* moments in your day. Imagine more and more moments of seeing the world through the eyes of the pure joyful energy of your Inner Being.

- See yourself busy, focused, and happy.

- See yourself experiencing a great-feeling *flow* in your days.

- See yourself having lots and lots of fun in your days.

- Imagine yourself living more and more in a huge "Happiness Expressway" throughout the day.

- See yourself moving through your day with the feeling of your *thriving/no-limits self*.

25

Great Things in Your Life

"And in that moment, I imagined the awesomeness of these wonderful things growing in my life."

Imagine great things in your life:

- clothes that look great on you

- interesting, fascinating, and even *inspiring* books

- fantastic music

- fun TV shows, inspiring TV shows

- enjoyable and super useful software (such as great apps on your phone)

- joy-giving household items (such as great-feeling pillows, decorations, furniture)

- a wonderful residence

- a vehicle you love

- more and more fun things to do in your life (Identify an activity in your life that is your most fun thing to do. Now imagine that all your activities in your week are that fun, or even more so.)

- fun and exciting hobbies, passions, projects

- Do free-form visualizing. In this practicing item, "stare off" and let your imagination go as you imagine all kinds of fantastic things in your life.

26

Better Feelings in Upcoming Days

> "And in that moment, I felt wonderful things
> ahead of me, and ahead of all of us."

- Think about various upcoming events in the next week or two. Then find your "happy spirit" for each of the events.

- See yourself feeling great at the end of today, tomorrow, and the next few days.

- Visualize a *blanket of joy* enveloping your whole upcoming week.

- See yourself in upcoming days as simply a deeply-happy human being.

Happy Images

*"And in that moment, I felt the power and joy
of these growing images in my life."*

- feeling free, like a kid on a bicycle

- a kid bouncing around and trying all kinds of fun and interesting things

- going down steps and feeling so light and happy

- puppies playing in the grass

- living in the day in a light way, as if I am a feather moving through the day

- a beautiful ballet dancer, moving lightly and swiftly, and soaring ever higher into the air

- happy sparkling energy all throughout my body

27 - Happy Images

- feeling more and more joy, alignment, and lightness in all the cells in my body

- experiencing waves and waves of happiness

- me lying in the grass, smiling and happy

- seeing myself with a rainbow appearing around me

- picturing myself in a small cabin by a lake in the south of France, very peaceful and happy

- so full of good energy, good cheer, and utter alignment that I only see good things in others

- walking into a room feeling great joy and so loving life

- seeing myself as a child growing into a magnificent being

- doors opening up... the seas parting... coming into a clearing

- a person whose pores are gradually opening up to let in more and more good energy

- a dam breaking loose

- Forrest Gump breaking out of his leg braces

- *waking up* feeling powerful

- eyes set back

- a clear and sure being

- a huge growing power in my chest

- like the Rock of Gibraltar, a rock in all circumstances

- a great leader who exudes alignment and clarity in all they do

- "She is always so clear-minded. She is following her own Vision."

- "He couldn't NOT take me." (woman auditioning)

- a startling person, who is so on top of things, and decisive and impeccable in all she does

- adding more weight to my exercise machine as I get stronger and stronger

- a magnificent runner, hitting my stride more and more

- ready-to-go energy: "Alright, team, let's go to work."

- "He simply does not get exhausted because he stays so aligned." (Others often find themselves running after him.)

27 - Happy Images

- generating a fantastic and powerful *current*, with a wake behind me

- she gets stuff done so easily and quickly because she has pre-paved ahead of time, and is therefore *so* ready to go

- the king of simple solutions

- me as a master craftsman, with every small movement being clear, competent, beautiful

- a sports team focused on a common vision and constantly finding a way to get around obstacles during the game

- a life filled with many exciting projects

- running through the airport talking on my cellphone and feeling so excited

- me as a kid seeing something I've been wanting arriving (for instance in the mail), and feeling such excitement

- feeling things clicking into place more and more

- feeling my whole mojo growing and growing

- exciting moments of *pouring it on and pouring it on and pouring it on*

- me having a powerful *engine* of great feelings that is growing bigger and bigger and bigger

- me as a locomotive coming down the tracks, building more and more momentum

- feeling great wellness in my being

- the feeling of a great and growing *foundation* in my life

28

Simply

"And in that moment, I just felt really good."

It doesn't matter what's happening around me.
It doesn't matter what the current physical details are.
It doesn't matter what others are saying or choosing.
It doesn't matter what my schedule for the day is.
It doesn't matter what day of the week it is, or what time it is.
None of this external stuff matters.
Because...

I am simply feeling better and better.

My days are becoming happier and happier.
I'm finding better and better flow in my days.
I am becoming more and more connected to Source Energy.
I am simply feeling more and more joyful in my days.

The cells in my body are getting healthier and healthier.
The cells in my body are having more and more fun.
The cells in my body are feeling more and more joy.
The cells in my body are simply feeling better and better.

I am finding a way to move *towards* more and more things in my life.
I am feeling the growing good energy of these things.
And I can feel its effect—so many things in my life are moving forward.
I am simply feeling more and more positive energy in my life.

My whole being is growing bigger and bigger.
My power is growing and growing.
I can feel my growing mojo in the things I do.
I am simply feeling more powerful in everything that I do.

I am so satisfied in so many places in my life.
I am having more and more fun in my life.
I am simply getting more and more excited about life.

29

Imagine

> "And in that moment, I imagined... and *felt*...
> whole new wonderful worlds."

- Imagine yourself as a newborn baby, feeling so happy, and feeling so excited about what is upcoming.

- Imagine yourself as a five-year-old in bed at night, feeling light and happy, and joyfully falling into a deep sleep.

- Imagine feeling a growing appreciation of *the wonderful cycles in life*... of exploring, of feeling a gap when I identify something I now want, and then joyfully aligning with what I want.

- Imagine a life of almost complete non-worry, of almost complete non-resistance.

- Imagine a life of feeling more and more confident at a core level, and moving around with lightness, happiness, and strength.

- Imagine the moment when it is time to transition out of your physical body... you are completely at peace, relaxed, fulfilled (for now!), and eager to experience the absolute joy of your next adventure.

30

You, *Amplified*

"And in that moment, I felt so alive...so myself... so *unlimited*."

- Be proud of unique *you*. You and your unique characteristics are not just a good thing—they are an infinitely great thing in this Universe.

- Imagine the freshness of a baby's joy and excitement in looking out into the world. Now imagine this is you, and imagine all that is before you.
"Oh, the places you'll go!" (Dr Seuss)

- You have so much to *be* and *do* and *have* and *give* in this world. What might that look like, and feel like?

- And now imagine "You, *Amplified*."
What might "You, Amplified" look like, and feel like?

- Consider your wildest, craziest, most exciting dream. Feel its possibility growing inside you.

- Imagine living an *exponential* life, a "life beyond words." What might this look like, and feel like?

- Practice the feeling of: "What an amazing world, and more and more I feel like I can do anything."

- Establish and glow who you are (to the ends of the earth).

Section 3 - Soothing

31

Soothing Path #1: Get Some Relief When You are Upset

Note: I am not a medical professional—this chapter simply describes a path that has helped me. The ideas are not meant, in any way, to supersede any guidance you are currently receiving from a professional.

When we are really upset and not thinking straight, we just want *relief*. What can we do?

Sometimes just stepping away or focusing elsewhere for a while is all we need to do. Other times we need more. We consider looking for positive aspects, but soon realize we are too upset. We just want to be *soothed*. The purpose of Soothing Path #1 is to soothe you when you are upset.

Soothing Path #1 steps:

1. Notice when you are feeling "off" as early as possible.
2. Stop and step away (when feasible).
3. Make feeling better your immediate priority.
4. Be quiet, take no action, come to no conclusions.
5. Take the hit, allowing yourself to feel whatever feelings are going on inside you.
6. Set the topic completely aside and ask "What better-feeling next step is available to me right now?"
7. Keep taking your next step (and just do the best you can).

Here are the details of those steps:

1. Notice When You are Feeling "Off" as Early as Possible

- *Notice when you are feeling "off" as early as possible. Then accept what's going on.* No one wants to feel "off" or in a bad mood. But if you are, you are, and the sooner you recognize it and accept it, the better. This step may be the most important one in the whole process, because if you can learn to recognize your "off" mood early on, before it gets really bad, then you will have far more leverage in pivoting to better-feeling thoughts. When you don't notice the bad feelings, or when you ignore them, the Law of Attraction will bring more bad feelings, which then will tend to continue to intensify until you finally decide to stop and find a better-feeling path.

- *Give yourself a break.* Guess what—we all have our moments! It is okay, and even expected, to have many different kinds of emotions in our journeys.

2. Stop and Step Away (When Feasible)

- *Stop what you are doing (when feasible).* It is not always easy to stop, but *stop*. And then...

- *Step away.* It can be helpful to move to a different location/environment.

3. Make Feeling Better Your Immediate Priority

- *Make feeling better your immediate priority.* How you feel is so important. If you are feeling bad, this means that you are less plugged into your core (good) energy! And it simply feels crappy—why spend any more moments in your life feeling bad than you need to?

4. Be Quiet, Take No Action, Come to No Conclusions

- *Be quiet.* Unless it feels inspired, do not interact with others. Sometimes when you are feeling crappy, it seems like other people caused your bad mood and it is tempting to have words with them. But if you interact with others from your current bad mood, it is likely the interactions will have bad results—a perfect match to your mood. So, as hard as it may be, say nothing and step away. If you feel that it would help to have a conversation, wait until later when you are in a better mood.

- *Take no action.* It can also be tempting to take action in order to immediately fix this. But if you take action from your current bad mood, the results will (again) be a match to your mood. If you feel that it would help to take action, wait until later when you are in a better mood.

- *Do no analysis, and do not come to any conclusions.* Right now you are not fully yourself, and you have a *highly skewed negative point of view.* Since you cannot see the topic clearly, this is not the time to analyze the topic, or come to any conclusions. Because if you do reach any conclusions about the topic, the conclusions will be bad—a perfect match to your mood. (And these will *not* be conclusions that your Inner Being agrees with.)

5. **Take the Hit, Allowing Yourself to Feel Whatever Feelings are Going On Inside You**

If you are just feeling "off" or a little cranky, this step does not apply to you, and you can proceed to #6 below. But if you are truly upset, this step is all about completely allowing yourself to *feel* whatever is going on inside you. Years ago, I went through a difficult time and had some very painful emotions, and as I tried to feel better, I fought and fought my bad feelings, but that only made it worse. So, if you are upset:

- *Know that whatever you are feeling is just fine.* It's okay, and it is temporary anyway.

- *Take the hit—fully allow yourself to feel any feelings going on inside you.* Mentally go inside, right to the place in your body where it feels like the bad emotions are (as best you can), and give yourself complete permission to feel whatever feelings are there. It can help to identify (and repeat) a word that describes your core feeling. While sometimes the feeling is vague, other times you'll be able to name the bad feeling, such as "scared," "discouraged," "disappointed," "ashamed," "frustrated," "angry," "furious," or "sad." Sometimes a more general term such as "stressed" or "hurting" best describes the feeling. If you can name the feeling, then it can help to internally repeat the word over and over for a minute or two, as you allow yourself to fully feel the feeling. An example is to say, "frustrated, frustrated, frustrated..." Other times, when the feeling is just some kind of vague bad feeling, focus inside your body where you have the bad feeling (as best you can) and allow yourself to simply feel whatever feelings are there.

- *Don't fight the bad feelings one iota.* Imagine you are a ragdoll, and just let everything go, where you no longer fight against *anything.*
  ... not fighting your mood in the least little bit
  ... not fighting the situation in the least little bit
  ... not fighting any events in the least little bit
  ... not fighting any physical discomfort in the least little bit
  ... giving up any and all "fighting against"
  Sometimes it can even help to say to the emotional (or physical) pain, "Hurt as much as you need to hurt."

- *Do not think about any details. At this point thinking about any details will only make you feel worse.* Just keep setting the details aside. No details, no analysis, no conclusions. Stay in your feelings, feel only your feelings.

- *For the couple minutes (or more) this will likely still hurt. But then...* After a bit, usually just a few minutes, you will likely find yourself feeling at least a little better. I have noticed that as I am letting the bad feelings be felt, they seem to gradually dissipate or "flow out of my body," almost as if I am letting air out of a pressurized balloon inside me. Consider how a young child experiences negative feelings. They feel them intensely, and then, often very quickly, they are simply *done*. They don't try to stop the bad feelings. They just feel them, and then go back to their habitual state of feeling good.

6. Set the Topic Completely Aside and Ask "What Better-Feeling Next Step is Available to Me Right Now?"

- *Now set the topic (problem area) completely aside.* When we are upset, we are frustrated. We want to fix the problem as quickly as possible, and then get back to our plans. *Stop.* Even though it is difficult, set the topic completely aside as best you can. (There may be nothing to set aside if you are simply in a bad mood. But sometimes when we are in a bad mood, there may be some specific issue going on underneath, and it can help to identify what is *really* bothering us. *Or* it may simply be because of the amount of internal "air time" we've lately been giving unhappy topics. You can shift this momentum by setting aside a few minutes in your days to focus on items in Chapters 19-30 or any other general good-feeling items/affirmations you might have.)

- *Ask: "What better-feeling next step is available to me right now?"* Turn your attention away from the topic and look for a small next step or activity that feels like it is anywhere in the direction of relief, even if it just a little relief. I sometimes look for a small better-feeling thought, or simply some kind of activity that is distracting and/or might stop the negative momentum.

- *Listen inside for anything in the direction of "better."* Taking a moment to listen inside is powerful in that you are proactively looking to your Inner Being to give you guidance. *This is the Inner Being that always knows a next step that would be helpful to you.* Listen for anything that feels like a good next step.

You might even say, "Inner Being, what do you suggest?" You may only get a slight impulse to do something—that's fine—move in that direction. This next step could be any number of things: a distracting/engaging activity, running errands, napping, taking a walk, listening to soothing words. The following three options often help:

+ Option 6.1: A Distracting/Engaging Activity

This is often the very first thing to do, as a completely different focus can significantly help in breaking the momentum. In this option, you completely distract yourself by doing some kind of busy activity, such as doing household tasks or running errands.

+ Option 6.2: Something Soothing

- Take a walk or go out in nature

- Take a nap

- Exercise

- Listen to music

- Do yoga

- Write in your journal

- Do a guided meditation

Soothing Path #1: Get Some Relief When You are Upset

- Listen to a seminar

- Read or listen to some soothing words. You may already have soothing words that have helped you in the past. You can also use one of the sets of soothing words found at the end of this chapter*.

- Just look for *one* better-feeling thought.

- Go more general in your thoughts. One process that can help with this is to read the first set of soothing words found at the end of this chapter*. Another path is to repeat a mantra. A mantra is helpful when you are so upset you can't seem to hold any kind of rational thought in your head. To help you identify a mantra, choose from the list of mantras found in Soothing Path #5.

- Quiet your mind. After you've calmed down a bit, some form of quieting-your-mind can help. This is about stopping active thoughts in whatever way you can, such as focusing on a simple sound you hear in your environment. This can be brief, as in 10-30 seconds, or longer, as in a few minutes on up to 20 minutes. When you do this, keep setting aside any thoughts about details from your life. This quieting-your-mind can also be in various formats. You might do this in a meditative pose or while going for a walk. If walking, consider quieting your mind for the next two or three blocks. You might then intersperse this with other soothing techniques, such as identifying positive aspects or thinking about feelings you *want*.

+ Option 6.3: A Light Focus on Something Positive (When Feeling a Little Better)

- Do your favorite, favorite activity. This can help you feel like yourself again.
- Make a list of the feelings you *want*.
- Slowly read through a list of positive emotion words, such as those found in Chapter 5.
- Lightly identify some positive things regarding the area that is bothering you.

I also use a couple of additional helpful techniques: *Rotations* and *Sequences*.

In a *Rotation,* you continually rotate (over a few hours) between doing an hour or more of a distracting/engaging activity (Option 6.1 above)—and doing brief (usually five minutes or less) soothing activities (Option 6.2 above). The idea of a Rotation is to keep distracting yourself *and* to keep interspersing this with tiny "injections" of soothing energies.

In a *Sequence,* you do a series of soothing/relaxing activities (once you have calmed down a bit). A Sequence normally requires you to get away from your normal activities for an hour or so. The idea of a Sequence is to take advantage of the Law of Attraction by steadily focusing, as best you can, on a *series* of soothing/relaxing activities (Option 6.2 above). One helpful sequence I do is to quiet my mind for 15-20 minutes, then listen to a few minutes of a seminar (such as an Abraham-Hicks workshop), and then have a beer while doing a relaxing activity. :)

7. Keep Taking Your Next Step (and Just Do the Best You Can)

- *Keep taking your next step (and just do the best you can).* Often we've been treating the situation as more serious than it really is—give yourself a break and just do the best you can.

- *Do not stare at the bad feeling or bad situation.* You might find yourself obsessively thinking about this awful thing. Try to ease back from this by *focusing elsewhere*, including doing activities and changing your environment.

- *Bad feelings often come in waves—it's okay and normal.* Just do the best you can from wherever you are in each moment, and then give yourself plenty of time to get back to feeling good again.

- *If need be, give yourself permission to be completely miserable for a while.* Sometimes whatever we do does not help—the bad feeling feels like a rock. If need be, allow yourself to be completely and utterly miserable for a while. Fortunately we do tend to cycle back to better feelings, but sometimes it takes a little while. When I have a bad feeling that is persisting, I find it helpful to think of it as a *fever*. We all know what it's like to have a fever—it feels bad but we also know it's just passing through. While it's here, let it be as crappy as it needs to be. In the meantime move forward in your day and focus on other activities as best you can.

Finally, if what is bothering you feels a bit bigger, Soothing Path #6 (Combine Soothing Paths) discusses how combining techniques over a period of days or weeks can be helpful.

* * *

*Soothing Words for Step 6.2 Above

"Read or listen to soothing words" is one of the activities mentioned under Option 6.2 above. Below are two streams of soothing words you might find helpful.

A Stream of Soothing Words to Help You Go More *General* in Your Thoughts

When you go more general in your thoughts, that lessens the resistance as it takes your mind away from any current bad-feeling details. Below is a simple path to help you do this.

You are likely starting from a place of thinking *specific* negative thoughts about the topic. Read the following statements, which are softer because they are *general* negative thoughts:

"I feel bad."
"I feel confused."
"I'm not sure where to go from here."
"I just don't feel great about the whole thing."

Soothing Path #1: Get Some Relief When You are Upset

As you stabilize in the above general negative thoughts, you can then start practicing general *positive* thoughts, as follows:

"Hmmm... I guess there are some aspects about this topic that are okay, maybe even some aspects that are good."
"And there may be other positive things I haven't thought of."
"Maybe a shift is possible."
"Maybe there is some hope here."
"I know that a lot of times things do work out."
"Well actually, most of the time things work out."
"I really don't have to have all the answers in this very moment."
"Once a little time passes, I'll probably feel a little better."
"And I'll probably be thinking more clearly too."
"I might even figure out something that will help."
"Maybe I'm closer to feeling better than I realize."
"I may actually only be a small tweak away from feeling better."
"I'm feeling a little more relaxed now."
"It will get sorted out."
"I think things will work out just fine."
"I'm starting to feel some optimism."
"I like the word 'optimism.'"
"I think I'll just focus on the word 'optimistic.'"
"optimistic... optimistic... optimistic..."

A Stream of Soothing Words to Slowly Read and Absorb

Slowly read and absorb the words in the following list. If you get to a phrase/statement that feels especially good, stop and read it a few more times, "milking it" for its good feelings.

- softer
- lighter
- letting go
- a little bit at a time
- a little better feeling
- giving it some time
- giving it as much time as it needs
- little improvements
- little improvements and finding my way
- passageways opening up

- Everything is going to be alright.
- It will be fine.
- I'm going to get through this.
- We're all going to get through this.
- It will work out.
- It will cycle.

- I think I'll lower the stakes.
- I think I'm not going to take things quite so seriously.
- I think I'll let up on the burden I'm putting on myself.
- I think I'll just let things unfold.
- Things have a way of working themselves out.

Soothing Path #1: Get Some Relief When You are Upset

- There is a path of relief for me.
- There is a path to feeling better.
- And whatever I'm feeling right now is fine.
- My feelings are temporary anyway.

- Some parts of this topic are already fine.
- Some parts of this topic are *good*.
- And having some glitches along the way is just fine.
- Glitches are part of this adventure called life.
- It is good that questions and choices arise along the way.
- Questions and choices really do add to my life—I would not want a life without them.
- This is a normal part of the cycle of growth, expansion, and improvement.
- This whole topic will serve me.

- There are many forces working on my behalf.
- My Inner Being is always with me.
- My Inner Being is there to guide me at each step.
- My Inner Being knows what to do.
- I'll keep listening to my Inner Being for my next step.

- I am where I am, and that's okay.
- I'm doing many things right.
- I'm doing just fine.
- I have a lot going for me.
- I have a good track record.

Section 3 - Soothing

- I've resolved many things before, and I can resolve this too.
- It's just a matter of shifting a few thoughts, and I can do that.

- I'm just going to take this one step at a time.
- The Universe always provides a next step.
- I'm going to keep gently listening inside.
- My only work is to keep finding my next better-feeling thought.
- I can relax and find one better-feeling thought.
- Over time, I can find more better-feeling thoughts.

- There *is* a solution.
- Maybe there is even a simple solution.
- The solution doesn't have to be either/or.
- I always have options.
- There are ongoing options for me.
- There are ongoing opportunities for me.

- It's all lined up, and it's all going to work out.
- There is a path for me.
- There is a *good* path for me.
- I like this unfolding path.
- I am figuring this out.
- I am good at doing what I set out to do.
- What I'm trying to do here is not so big.
- I'm just going to keep relaxing and releasing this to the Universe.

Soothing Path #1: Get Some Relief When You are Upset

- I am on track.
- I'm getting there.
- The progress I've made is *real*.

- I am on my path.
- I am on a good path.

- I can find my power in all of this.
- I can make more choices.
- It feels good to realize I can make more choices.
- I can choose to focus on the parts of my life that feel good.
- And I can choose what I focus on when I think about this topic.
- There are some good things to think about for this topic.
- I can take the lead in this.
- I am a leader.
- More and more, I am the leader of my life.

- I can have fun with this.
- Maybe I can even thrive here.
- I'm growing in my confidence.
- I can do this.
- I am strong.
- I really am getting there.
- *I've got this.*

And so...

- Everything is going to be alright.
- "Okay-ness" is just fine for now.
- It really is getting better.
- I am in a good place.
- My well-being is assured.
- All our well-beings are assured.
- All is well.

Soothing Path #2: Set the Topic Aside for a While

Have you ever given up on finding something that is lost... only to then find it? Have you ever given up on some problem... only to then find a solution? Have you ever known a couple who were trying to get pregnant for months or years, who then finally gave up and adopted... only to then get pregnant?

Many people have had this experience where they finally "gave up" on something they were struggling with, and then they found a solution, sometimes immediately. This occurs because when our thoughts are in an overwhelming PROBLEM/STRUGGLE/CAN'T-SOLVE-THIS feeling, and then we finally give up that struggle, the blocking focus/energy seems to get "freed" or "released." In effect, we let go of some kind of internal resistance that is blocking what we want from coming to us. So the "giving up" is really about giving up the *resistance* about what's going on. It turns out that often the easiest way to get rid of this blocking energy is to completely set aside the topic for a while. But how do we set aside a topic that currently feels so big in our thoughts?

First of all, stop what you are doing... breathe... take a break.

It is not always easy to stop when we are so engrossed in something. But make a decision to stop for a moment. When feasible, move to a different room or environment. Initiate a new activity. Take a walk, take a nap, whatever. This new location or activity can help you get out of your immediate "tunnel" of obsessive thoughts. This might be for a few minutes, an hour, or a day. That may be all you need to do to release the resistance.

If the resistance persists, consider setting aside the topic for a longer period of time. You can do this by (habitually) directing your attention to other areas in your life.

Since you cannot really "not think about that thing you're thinking about," the key is to focus elsewhere in both your thoughts and your activities. Focus on the rest of your life for a while.

Because you are starting with a momentum of frequently thinking about this topic, it may take some persistence in focusing elsewhere. But as you *activate* your thoughts about other areas in your life, it will get easier and easier to move on from the topic.

Our goal is to get to a place where we are truly not "on the channel" of that topic anymore, where we have completely let it go, released the whole thing.

Soothing Path #2: Set the Topic Aside for a While

But what if this topic is very "present" in your life?

Sometimes we are not in a place where we can completely set a topic aside since it is so physically present in our lives. Maybe we are struggling with our job, someone we live with, or our body. Other times we struggle to set the topic aside simply because the topic feels so big inside us.

Start by setting an *intention* to set the topic aside. After you've set this intention, here are some ideas on how to actually set the topic aside:

1. *Lower your whole intensity around the topic.* By ratcheting down your whole energy around the topic, you start to open yourself up to relief, to being able to breathe again.

2. *Lower the stakes.* The situation is often not as critical as we've been making it out to be; we often have more leeway than we realize. And "we cannot get it wrong because it is never done." (Abraham)

3. *Go general regarding the topic.* Decide to live in the best *general* good-feeling place about the topic that you can find. This might be a general "I'm going to choose to have faith here, as best I can, and give this some time." Or it might simply be a best-general-feeling-I-can-find about the topic. Or it might be to practice a mantra such as "it will work out." And when you do this, keep setting aside thinking about details; keep them intentionally *fuzzy* and *out-of-focus*.

4. *When feasible, make the topic less physically present in your life.* Sometimes there are simple things you can do to have the topic less physically present in your life, so that you simply see and/or interact with the topic less. These physical changes should not be your main focus in trying to feel better about the topic, but sometimes there are a few things you can do that can help. As an example, if you are trying to practice better feelings about a person, sometimes it can help to simply be with the person less for a while. This does not mean you do not care about them. In fact, you are doing this *because* you care about them—getting some time away can help you reset yourself into being more of your whole (good-feeling) self when you are with them. As another example, if you are practicing a new internal image for your body (such as when trying to lose weight), consider removing your scale or even mirrors from your daily spaces.

5. *Focus elsewhere in your life more, as best you can.* You very likely have other good things going on in your life. Spend more time focusing on these other areas. The more you can engage and create in these other areas, the better.

6. *Activate more of YOU.* Sometimes it seems like there is too much of the resistant topic in your life. But the real problem is there is not enough of YOU. That is, there is not enough of CONNECTED YOU. Consider practicing more feelings of *the Real You*. Remember who you really are. Remember the true huge joy at your core. Remember that at your core, you are one who creates and thrives. Practice more of the feelings

Soothing Path #2: Set the Topic Aside for a While

of the Real You in your daily life. You can also use Section 2 in this book to remind yourself of these feelings.

Finally, once you are ready to address the topic again, consider starting up with some brief practicing of (general) better feelings about the topic. Chapters 3-13 can help with this.

Soothing Path #3: Write Downstream Thoughts about the Topic (or) Do the Focus Wheel Process

This chapter presents two ways to focus on the positive aspects of a topic. The first one is called Downstream Thoughts and focuses on positive aspects of the *overall* topic (vs the particular area that is bothering you). This is a general, and therefore less resistant, way to positively focus on a topic. The second one is Abraham-Hicks's Focus Wheel process, which can help you get relief in the exact area that is bothering you. I have found both processes to be helpful, depending on the circumstance. Choose between the two based on which one feels better in the moment.

Sometimes doing a process, such as the ones in this chapter, does not fully resolve your negative feelings. That's ok—if you felt *any* better feeling, the process has moved you forward. Furthermore, when this happens, you might find that a day or two later you have new insights and find relief "out of the blue." This is often because your feelings had indeed improved to some extent when doing the process, which then allowed you to later let in additional relief, insights, or solutions. The Soothing Path #6 chapter (Combine Soothing Paths) gives an example of this.

Downstream Thoughts

Many times over the course of the last few years, I have gone into my den, sat down on the couch, and written this phrase at the top of a piece of paper: "D.T." This stands for "Downstream Thoughts," a helpful phrase coined by Abraham. The word "downstream" refers to the fact that it is much easier to swim downstream than upstream. Here is how I use that term in this "Downstream Thoughts" process: For a troublesome topic, rather than focusing on what you are struggling with (the more difficult *upstream* part of the topic), this process focuses on thoughts that feel good about the *overall* topic (the easier *downstream* part of the topic). What I like about this process is that it is light-feeling and easy to do, and at the same time can be powerful in helping us improve our feelings about the overall topic. It's a way to gently—without a lot of struggle—help one feel better about the topic.

I use this process in two different circumstances: when something specific is bothering me, and when I feel crappy in general and I just want to get my whole self back to feeling good.

When you do this process, you are beginning from a place of resistance. That means you have some negative momentum going on inside you. So when you begin the process, be patient, giving it time as you try to identify your first neutral or better-feeling thought. Note that I included the word "neutral." Sometimes the best one can do for the first few statements is to write down neutral-feeling thoughts. That is fine—at least these are not the negative thoughts you had been thinking! And then, bit by bit, you can move into writing thoughts that feel better and better.

Soothing Path #3: Write Downstream Thoughts (or) Do a Focus Wheel

As you try to think of statements (or phrases), let each one be something that you actually feel. Write down anything that feels good, even good *feelings* (such as "ease"). Feel free to also stray into other topics in your life, as long as you're writing words that feel good.

It can also help to periodically *read* the statements you've written so far—this helps cement and expand your current positive momentum. This process is really about the Law of Attraction in action, as writing down a few neutral or slightly better-feeling thoughts tends to relax you, and tends to open up your mind to more substantial better-feeling thoughts.

In doing this process, don't write down any thoughts that "should" feel good but actually don't. The criteria is based solely on how it *really* feels to you. For instance, if you have an elderly parent who is not well and is suffering, one of your siblings might say their positive thought is that the parent could recover. But for you, the thought that gives you the most relief is "they could die (and no longer suffer)." If a thought gives you any kind of relief, write it down, because any thought that feels better is a thought worth noting.

A couple more points: As you write down better-feeling aspects of the topic, consider circling any items that feel particularly good, so they stand out and can be used for later practicing. Additionally, once you are done with the list, it can be helpful to re-read the words so you can again absorb the better feelings of the words.

Variation #1: Take a walk and talk to yourself (possibly out loud) about some of the reasons why this will have a happy ending.

> **Variation #2:** You might think of this variation as an *extended* version of the Downstream Thoughts process. After you do the initial Downstream Thoughts process, consider keeping the list around and adding to it throughout the day or on following days. This can become your cumulative, ongoing list.

The Focus Wheel Process (from Abraham-Hicks)

The Focus Wheel process is another powerful way to soothe a topic that is bothering you. In comparison to the Downstream Thoughts process, this one focuses on giving you relief right in the area where you are struggling most. While this process is helpful in many circumstances, if it feels like too specific a focus on your sorest spot, then consider doing the Downstream Thoughts process instead.

When you do the Focus Wheel process, don't do it for the purpose of making some result happen in your life. Do it solely because it will help you feel better. Do it for the pleasure of writing down, one by one, statements that nudge you toward better and better feelings.

The first step in the process is to identify what is most bothering you about the current situation. In other words, identify your core bad feeling regarding this topic. Many times this is obvious, but on occasion, once we think about it, we realize that what is *really* bothering us is something different than what we had first thought. It is not necessary to write this down, but mentally identifying it gives you a clear starting place, and it will help you more clearly *feel* the improvement as you find your way to better and better feelings.

Soothing Path #3: Write Downstream Thoughts (or) Do a Focus Wheel

Next take a piece of paper and draw a circle in the center of the page. In that circle write a statement that describes what you most want. Focus on the *feeling* you want rather than the physical results you want. The goal is to write a statement that describes a good feeling that would soothe or resolve your sorest-spot feeling. *At this point, the statement you write down will not yet feel true.*

Then, like the numbers on a clock, draw 12 small circles around the center circle. In the 12 o'clock circle, write something *you already believe* that in any way evokes any of the good feeling of the statement you wrote in the center circle. (Make sure to only write down statements that actually feel better, not ones that are "supposed" to feel better.) Next write another better-feeling statement in the 1 o'clock circle, and then in each of the remaining circles of the clock. You may not be able to find 12 statements, but find as many as you can. As you do this, sometimes it helps to re-read the statements you've written so far, which can help grow your better-feeling momentum. In fact, after you are done, re-read the full list of statements, along with the statement in the center, so you can further absorb the good feelings of the words. You may feel a complete resolution of your feelings, or you may just feel somewhat better. Even if your feelings are not completely resolved, if you have moved even a little towards better feelings, you have been successful in the process, as you have moved forward in positively shifting your feelings around this topic.

Here's an example of a Focus Wheel: Let's say you are frustrated in your job because you feel your boss does not appreciate your work. You identify what you *don't* want as: "My boss does not appreciate the work I do." In the center circle on the page you write the feeling you *do* want as: "**I feel appreciated by my boss at work.**" Below are some statements you might write in the clock positions. Again, these are statements you already believe that evoke some of the feeling of the statement in the center of the page:

- My boss does not appear to give many compliments to *anyone*.
- My boss does compliment me every once in a while.
- My boss gives me good reviews.
- My boss gives me important assignments, and I realize she does that because she thinks I do a good job and am reliable.
- My co-workers appreciate and respect my work.
- I know I do a good job.
- When I am in a good mood, I don't think about, or worry about, what my boss or others think because I feel so good.
- I now realize that it is on days when I'm in a sketchy mood that I feel most in need of praise from my boss.
- If I do more to make sure I stay in a good mood, I won't care so much about what my boss or others say or do.
- I can do that – I can do more to stay more connected at work.
- I like that idea.
- I think my boss probably appreciates me more than I realize, and now I know that what *really* matters is for me to be in a good mood at work!

In writing down each of the 12 statements, you are increasingly *activating* the better feelings associated with the "what you *do* want" statement in the center circle. In this example you started out by identifying some better-feeling statements around that specific topic. However, you started to realize the additional importance of staying in a good mood at work. These combined statements helped you feel better about your job overall, along with also feeling more appreciated at work.

There are additional examples of this process in the Soothing Path #6 chapter. Various people on the Internet have also described this process in articles and YouTube videos.

34

Soothing Path #4: Identify the Feelings You *Want* for a Topic—and Then Keep Focusing There, Focusing There, Focusing There

Note: A variation of this process is also found in Chapter 4 ("The Feelings You Want for This Topic"). This is because focusing on the feelings you want can be helpful both when one is feeling good about a topic and when one is feeling resistance.

When we are troubled by a topic, we are of course focusing on bad-feeling aspects of the topic. In this state, we can get into such an all-consuming "tunnel" that these bad-feeling aspects can feel like they are the *only* aspects of the topic. The process in this chapter helps us focus on much-better-feeling parts of the topic, specifically the feelings we *want* for the topic.

In this process we don't try to do any fixing of the jumble of worrisome thoughts—we simply check out of that game. We do this by asking, "What are the feelings I *want* for this topic?" Because we've been focusing on the bad-feeling aspects of the topic, this new positive focus can feel fresh and invigorating. In the words of Abraham, this is about "dreaming everything new."

Now, list feelings you want related to this topic. This is not about physical things you want. Just list feeling after feeling, such as "ease, fun, flow, happiness, excited, an overall good feeling."

At first it might feel like you are just writing words down. *But as you write, try to find the feeling behind the words.* When you do this, your feelings, in an almost primitive manner, tend to move into better-feeling places.

As you are writing, if you feel the power of some particular word, consider writing it more than once. For example, if you have just written the word "fun" and you realize that the idea of fun particularly resonates with you, write the word "fun" over and over.

List feelings as long as it feels good.

Sometimes, for more difficult topics, it can also help to repeat this process on multiple days (from scratch). Doing this helps you *tune yourself*, day by day, to the vibration of the feelings you want.

Doing this process by physically writing the words is an excellent way to focus your mind. However, there are additional helpful ways to do this process. For example, I have often found great benefit in doing this in my mind (or out loud) while taking a walk. Other methods can be used too, as in the following example.

One day a few years ago, I accepted a job. I did not see it as some ideal job, but it felt like a good next job for me. A day later (before I had started the new job), I got a call from a recruiter who let me know about another job, a job that appeared to be better than the one I had accepted. So I asked the recruiter to submit my resume for the new job. After I hung up the phone, this immediately bothered me. As in *really* bothered me. I wanted it to be okay for me to at least find out whether this new job was indeed a better job for me. But I felt really bothered by what I had done and wasn't sure how

Soothing Path #4: Identify Feelings You Want—and Then Keep Focusing There

to process it. So, I thought, "Well, I'll go to the gym and maybe that distraction will help me sort this out." At the gym I was still struggling. And then, while exercising on the elliptical machine, I thought, "I'll just focus on the feelings I *want*." And I focused on thoughts such as "alignment, joy, happiness, feeling good, happy ending." For about 5-10 minutes I just focused and focused and focused on general positive-emotion words such as these. After I'd done this a while, I began to feel some relief. Then I felt more and more relief, and then shortly a *flood* of relief. I felt aligned and joyous and life was wonderful. The other thing I felt was clarity. I felt absolutely clear what I should do—I should call up the recruiter for the new opportunity and tell him "never mind." That is what I did, and it felt perfect. I am not saying this would have been the right decision for anyone else. It was simply the right decision for me that day. And the point is not what I decided. The point is *I found a path to relief.* And I found it by focusing on the feelings I wanted. As it turned out, the job I actually took ended being a great job!

35

Soothing Path #5: Practice a Soothing *Mantra* for the Topic

A few years ago, I was in a 7-Eleven convenience store and a man burst into the store, announcing there was someone in the parking lot with a gun who was threatening to kill some guy. Wow. In processing this, I realized that the very best thing I could do was keep myself in the best-feeling place I could. So I thought of the words "happy ending" and kept saying that to myself, "happy ending... happy ending... happy ending." I also decided to stay in line and continue to check out. Then I chose to simply go to my car. That was in fact the anticlimactic ending of the whole experience—I never saw the man with the gun. From an Action Hero standpoint, it was a disappointing ending. From a "I want to feel good" standpoint, it was a fantastic ending. I had found a way, just by repeating a soothing mantra, to keep myself in a good-feeling place, and I believe that helped me avoid interacting with the man.

Another time, I was on a guided bicycle tour in Idaho, and one day I had gone "all out" on my bike. When I finished, I could tell I was exhausted and dehydrated. As I rested and drank fluids, I became really concerned, wondering if I had pushed too hard. I was getting some relief with the rest and fluids, but I was still struggling. I happened to think of the sentence, "There is wellness inside my body." I found that phrase so soothing. So, for the next 20-30 minutes, while I rested and drank, I kept repeating those words to myself, "There is wellness inside my body... there is wellness inside my body... there is wellness inside my body..." Hearing the words over and over really soothed me, and I steadily kept feeling better and better. I soon fully recovered.

The above examples show how, when we are uncertain or scared, we often cannot "positive think" our way to feeling better. In these kinds of situations, just repeating one simple better-feeling mantra, over and over, can greatly soothe us.

While the above are smaller examples of the power of a mantra, mantras can also be helpful with much larger worrisome topics. For big-feeling topics, there can be a tendency to obsessively worry about the topic all day and, as stated, trying to find positive thoughts in the midst of lots of troubling thoughts can be difficult. This is where mantras can help, mantras such as "Everything is going to be alright," "It will work out," or simply "There IS a path for me." *Repeating a mantra that feels even a little better is much, much better than haphazardly worrying about a topic all day long.*

Here are the guidelines to using this technique:

- *Find a phrase, sentence, or image that feels better in any regard.* It does not matter why a particular thought feels better. If it helps you feel even a little better, it is worth using, since (at the very least) it stops your rush of bad-feeling thoughts. And from there it can then grow into even more significant better feelings.

Soothing Path #5: Practice a Soothing Mantra for the Topic

- *Repeat it over and over, setting aside all other thoughts.* Repeating the mantra is what allows its good feeling to gradually "take over" your internal feeling-space. If it continues to feel good, consider taking it with you to use as your new phrase for next few hours or days. Use it as long as it helps you feel better. You can think of this as your new "simple focus" for the topic.

On the next few pages are some sample mantras. Look for any statement, phrase, or image that resonates with you.

Section 3 - Soothing

Statements

- Everything is going to be alright.
- It's going to get better.
- It's getting better.
- There's nothing serious going on here.
- It's all small stuff.
- It will be fine.

- Things have a way of working themselves out.
- It will work out.
- It will all work out.
- It always works out for me.
- I'm going to choose to have faith.
- I think I'll just relax, and listen for a while.

- There is relief available to me.
- My Inner Being can help me.
- There is a solution.
- There is a path for me.
- There is a *good* path for me.
- There is a path of relief for me.

- This will serve me.
- Every bit of this will serve me.
- This will lead to something good.
- Whatever is happening will lead me in a good direction.
- I am finding my place with this.
- I'm doing just fine.

Soothing Path #5: Practice a Soothing Mantra for the Topic

- I'm doing really well.
- I am on track.
- I am on my path.
- I am on a good path.
- I am on the right path.
- The progress I've made is *real*.

- I'm getting there.
- Things are fine.
- Everything is on track.
- It is all working together.
- There is wellness inside my body.
- There is great health in my body.

- The world is a good place.
- There is great wellness in this world.
- There are so many things going well.
- There are many good things in this life.
- There are many good things in my life.
- So much is going right in my life.

- I'm doing so many things right.
- Overall things are fine/good.
- It doesn't have to be perfect.
- I am really good at finding my way to a solution.
- I can figure this out.
- I'll figure this out.
- I'm going to figure this out.
- I'm going to get there.

- I can do this.
- I can align with this.
- It doesn't have to be either/or.
- *I have choices.*
- I've got this.
- I can thrive here.

Phrases

- a little bit better, a little bit better, a little bit better
- better, better, better
- getting better, getting better, getting better
- just my next step, just my next step, just my next step
- all in good time, all in good time, all in good time
- a good feeling, a good feeling, a good feeling (no details)
- let go, let go, let go
- let it go, let it go, let it go
- optimistic, optimistic, optimistic
- solutions, solutions, solutions (the whole general feeling of *solutions*)
- well-being, well-being, well-being
- core good health inside me, core good health inside me, core good health inside me
- my growing mojo, my growing mojo, my growing mojo
- my core power, my core power, my core power
- the Real Me, the Real Me, the Real Me
- my Vision, my Vision, my Vision

Soothing Path #5: Practice a Soothing Mantra for the Topic

- my Inner Being, my Inner Being, my Inner Being (the bigger part of you that feels pure positive feelings)
- simply happy, simply happy, simply happy
- quick and easy resolution, quick and easy resolution, quick and easy resolution
- happy ending, happy ending, happy ending
- It can also feel good to choose a word or phrase for your mantra that describes a simple positive emotion. An example is "love, love, love." Two sources for positive-emotion words are Chapter 4 ("The Feelings You Want for This Topic") and Chapter 5 ("Positive Emotions").

Images

- Imagine you feeling good at the end (for whatever reason).
- Imagine an image of where you want to be. (One day years ago, I was headed home from a business trip, and *really* wanted to be home. I knew all of my flight connections would be close, so I kept imagining me sitting in my easy chair that evening. And that was exactly the result.)
- an image of you as a connected 5-year-old (feeling light and happy, and feeling excited about almost everything)
- an image of you as a connected 18-year-old (feeling your fantastic health and great energy and excitement about life)
- (See also Chapter 27 "Happy Images")

Many of the above items have soothed me at one time or another, but I wanted to make special mention of a few of them. Recently I was having troubling thoughts about some things going on in the world, and I found the following statements to be particularly soothing: "The world is a good place" and "There is great wellness in this world." Additionally, sometimes when I wake up in the morning, I like to use the phrase "I'm doing really well," which can be a helpful way to start one's day.

36

Soothing Path #6: Combine the Above Paths for an Extra Powerful Breakthrough

There is great power in soothing a topic from multiple directions, and doing it over a few hours or a few days.

What do you do when you have a topic that feels so bad that you almost cannot imagine feeling good about it? Maybe you've even tried a soothing process, but the topic feels so "off" or "intractable" that it feels like the process barely scratched the surface of helping you truly feel better. When you have this kind of topic, consider doing a series of soothing processes over a period of a few hours or a few days. This takes soothing to whole new powerful levels. This chapter will discuss some ways to do this, and some things to keep in mind as you go.

Where do you start? No matter where you are in your journey, always begin by listening inside for anything that feels like a good next step. It is worth taking the time to do this, as your *feeling* about any potential next step represents guidance from your Inner Being. Note that the feeling/impulse may be only a *slight* feeling/impulse—that's ok, as even a slightly positive feeling about a potential step is an indication that this step will move you in the right direction.

Here are a few pointers in this step-by-step journey of soothing yourself:

- *Your immediate goal should be to go from upset to less upset.* When you are upset, you might be tempted to look for something that will quickly solve the whole problem. But when you are upset, that is too big a jump. Instead focus only on going from *upset* to *less upset*. That is your easiest path to relief.

- *It can help to stay in a more general feeling-place about this topic for a while.* Set an intention to keep your mind in a more *general* feeling-place for this topic for a while. Decide to keep current details *fuzzy and out-of-focus*, and to also think of them as *temporary and unimportant*.

> For really big-feeling topics, a helpful path can be: 1) Stay general (no details) in your thoughts about the topic, and 2) Focus only on a chosen mantra (see Soothing Path #5), such as "It will work out." Big-feeling topics take time to shift, and this simple approach of "living in" a good-feeling mantra day after day (while staying out of the details) can have a powerful osmosis effect.

- *There are clues all around you.* Your Inner Being is always giving you clues for helpful next steps. These clues are fine-tuned for you specifically, as your Inner Being knows what next steps are best for *you*, given current circumstance and your beliefs. These clues are always available to each of us. To hear them,

Soothing Path #6: Combine Paths for an Extra Powerful Breakthrough

all you need to do is... distract yourself a little... lighten up your mood a little... give yourself a break a little... soothe yourself a little... practice the feelings you want a little. Then you will start to hear the voice of your Inner Being. You get impulses. You hear "come over here." You hear "you're getting warmer/colder." As you start to hear clues you realize, more and more, that your Inner Being is always by your side, offering assistance to help you in *anything* you are experiencing, and it is up to each of us to tune into those clues. Which leads us to...

- *"Listen instead of talk." - Abraham* As we are listening for guidance for a helpful next step, it is important that we mainly focus on relaxing and then *listening*. Many of us have lots of self-talk and "shoulds" running through our minds. This is often our conscious brain talking, trying to logically figure things out. But instead of talking, do whatever you can to relax more and listen inside, which will allow your Inner Guidance a chance to point you in the direction of a helpful next step. And in this whole process...

- *"Let it come to you." - Abraham* Let any impulses and/or results come to you—don't try to go out and "make" something happen. The key is to keep looking for small steps as you build a better and better atmosphere of thoughts and feelings.

* * *

Section 3 - Soothing

Here is a recent example from my life, which is lengthy but I believe instructive in multiple ways. It is not about a major life issue, but it provides an example of an emotional journey, and the kind of feelings and questions that can arise along the way.

A few weeks ago, I was looking for a specific type of journaling/diary phone app, but was having trouble finding one that matched my criteria. I had emailed the company of one of the apps, asking about the app's capabilities, and got a quick and helpful response. However, I was still unsure about whether to proceed with the app and was feeling impatient. At some point in this impatient and frustrated state of mind, I went ahead and ordered a trial subscription. By the next day, I had tried it out and realized this app was not for me. I also was aware I had only three days to cancel my trial subscription, so I sent the company an email requesting the cancellation. Since it was the weekend, I did not get a response until Monday, and the email said the company could not cancel it—I would have to do it in the App Store. So I pulled out my phone, tried that, and found something that *maybe* did it, but it was unclear, and I did not have a good feeling about it. And guess what? Just like that, later that day I was charged $29.99. Grrrr... yep, this was a match to the impatient and frustrated state of mind I was in when I ordered the trial subscription. Argh... now what?

I took a break for a day or two to calm down, but I was not happy. However, I did do one thing right; instead of immediately sending the company an email from my still-frustrated state (which in my agitated state I really, really wanted to do), I decided to do a Focus Wheel **(Soothing Path #3)**. In the Focus Wheel, the bad feeling I identified was that I was unfairly charged $29.99. I then tried to identify what I most wanted. Of course what I most wanted was

Soothing Path #6: Combine Paths for an Extra Powerful Breakthrough

to get my money back! But, in my current state, that felt almost impossible. I also realized that what I always want in life, no matter the particular experience, is to feel emotionally good—that is what we all ultimately seek in everything we do. I thought that, when this whole thing is done, I just want to somehow feel good about the whole thing. So the statement I wrote in the center of the page was **"I have a good feeling about this app purchase experience."** I could have instead written down "I will get my money back," but again that felt almost impossible, and really resistant. And, as stated, my goals have become more focused on *having good feelings* rather than getting specific physical results, so the statement aligned with those goals. Note that, as is normal when doing a Focus Wheel, when I first wrote down my statement of "I have a good feeling about this app purchase experience," I definitely did not (yet) feel that way, but it felt that it might eventually be possible.

Below are some of the statements I wrote in the clock positions on the page. Per the Focus Wheel instructions, I only wrote down statements *I already believed* that felt at least a little better.

- The customer service person was nice in her original email.
- They probably have lots of happy customers.
- I could be one too.
- I have good energy overall.
- There IS a path for me.
- There is a GOOD path for me.
- The website of the app is very professional.
- It is clear they have good intentions.
- I just want a good feeling, and I can find that.
- The customer service person did answer my email.

- We've had very nice communications so far.
- Later today I can do more practicing of the feelings I want.

The process was done, and I felt at least a little better. Then I immediately had the inspiration to simply write down some of the feelings I *want* **(Soothing Path #4)** for this topic. I did so as follows: "happy, connected, aligned, good feeling, nice people (them and me), it's okay, it will work out, we'll get there, a good feeling."

I noticed that the last item, "a good feeling," immediately struck a chord with me, so I circled the item. My feelings were not yet resolved, but I did feel better to some extent.

Then I decided that for a day or two, "a good feeling" would be my mantra **(Soothing Path #5)** for this topic. And I used that mantra over the next few days whenever I thought about this topic.

I was feeling somewhat better, but since I still didn't really feel like writing another email to the company, I trusted my feelings and waited. I knew I could do another Focus Wheel. But since the whole topic continued to feel somewhat unpleasant, I just did nothing, and there it sat for about 10 days. I did not force anything.

Then one day I was at home at around 3:00 in the afternoon. I had an hour and a half before something I needed to do at 4:30, so I said to the Universe, "For the next 90 minutes, I just want to feel good." I decided I would listen to my Inner Guidance and do whatever feels best in the moment.

I have done this before and typically feel subtle leanings to do some particular thing. And in line with that, first I felt like cleaning our robot vacuum cleaner. Then I did some other stuff around the house. Then all of a sudden I had an inspiration to do a Focus Wheel

Soothing Path #6: Combine Paths for an Extra Powerful Breakthrough

about the app topic. This was truly out of the blue, as I had had no thought of doing this process for this topic.

I began by writing down the same statement at the center of the page, **"I have a good feeling about this purchase experience"** and then wrote the following statements around it:

- I found a good feeling previously.
- I like that I clearly recognized that, in the moment when I signed up, it was from a place of resistance.
- I like that moving on in my life (after I check with the company one last time) feels pretty easy. (I had started to reconcile myself with moving on.)
- I like that I may learn something great based on this experience.
- The customer support person did actually respond previously.
- I like that I can write my new email from my new better-feeling place.
- I like that I'm listening inside as I go.
- There *is* a solution of good feelings.

And then all of a sudden (right in the middle of the Focus Wheel process), I had a clear inspiration to set aside the paper and go to the app company's website on my computer. I had been to this website before, and it appeared to confirm that the company cannot do refunds. Yet, I could tell in doing the Focus Wheel that I was feeling better, and from that good-feeling place I simply followed this strong impulse. On the website, I saw the same support pages I had seen before, but then I had an idea to click some of the other links. One of these triggered the opening of the iTunes application on my computer. I looked around, and saw a link to an area that lists all of your iPhone purchases. I went there, saw my $29.99 purchase, and lo and behold there was a button to request a refund. I clicked it. A couple days later I got my refund. Yeahhh!

As you could see, this ended up being quite the journey. It felt great at the end and felt so worth it! I had shown myself I could find a solution by having a singular goal of trying to feel better, and by doing the patient one-better-feeling-at-a-time work. One of the funny things about this is that, when it was all over, I realized it would make a great example for the book, and I had to fetch my first Focus Wheel paper out of the garbage! (How did it happen to work out, that when I was writing this last part of the book, that this helpful example of Soothing Path #6 happened to me? All I can say is "there goes the Universe again.") Besides the pointers mentioned at the beginning of this chapter, here are a few additional takeaways from this experience:

- I maintained a clear goal of just feeling better in any way I could. While certainly I wanted to get my money back, I just kept focusing on feeling better. Of course focusing on finding better *feelings* is in fact our most direct path to getting good-feeling *results*!

- When we do a soothing process, if it doesn't get us to a full resolution (as in the first Focus Wheel above), it is tempting to say we were not successful. But if we have stabilized or positively moved our feelings at all, we absolutely were successful. Which leads us to...

Soothing Path #6: Combine Paths for an Extra Powerful Breakthrough

- It is helpful to maintain a "present-moment-ness" in figuring out each next step along the way. In each moment I simply asked, "What feels better right now?" Then I listened inside. I did not force things in a certain direction, and I did not get ahead of myself.

- As we grow in our ability to find better feelings when something throws us off, we grow a key ability in life, as this is such a large part of our life journey. The journey is: We experience contrast. If need be, we "take the hit" of feeling the gap between what we want and what we have. We then find a way to redirect ourselves towards the feelings we *want*, which soon gives us our first manifestation (better feelings). We then continue to look for better and better feelings. Then any physical manifestations that are a match to our improved feelings follow.

37

Closing Thoughts

Thank you for taking this journey with me. Have you found a path for your own daily practicing of better feelings? As long as your practicing feels good, you are doing something of benefit for yourself. You are also making a daily statement of *intention*. You are saying,

This is the direction I am leaning.
This is the direction I am practicing.
This is the direction I am growing.

So just keep "punching the clock" of practicing better feelings, day after day. Let this practice be a rock in your life. Fuss less about what is happening around you, setting aside thoughts about trying to get others to cooperate or understand. Keep practicing and building your *own* powerful good feelings, which will then allow you to be that centered and happy person who thrives and powerfully influences everyone around them.

Wishing you well!

Acknowledgements

First of all, thank you to Esther Hicks, Jerry Hicks, and Abraham, whose examples and words have helped me (and many people throughout the world). Their teachings are joyful and immensely practical. Their website is www.abraham-hicks.com.

Thanks also to Karen Williams, who, first of all, provided expert guidance and editing assistance. She has a fantastic understanding of the Law of Attraction, and has many helpful tools and books available via her website (www.karenmoneywilliams.com). Thanks again to both Karen and her beau Mark, who have hosted weekly LOA meetings at their home (and helped many people) for years. Special thanks to them for continuing to believe in me and my quest to create helpful tools for others.

Also thanks to Josephine Ferguson and Mary Scott (my other two expert editors/reviewers), and to Danielle Smith-Boldt for her wonderful cover design.

Thank you also to my Mom and Dad, who loved me unconditionally and supported me, even in my forays into "what's he doing now?" paths. I so appreciate that you allowed me to find and be myself.

I'd also like to thank my friend, Rand Hoyt. For a number of years, he was my "partner in crime" in doing workshops to help others connect with their passions in life. It was during the fun times we had when I first thought of collecting tools for a book. Thank you, Rand, for being such a good friend for so many years.

Finally, thank you to my wife, Mary Lou, who has been my partner and best friend across so many years and adventures. Thank you for sharing your great spirit with me, and for being my co-creator and joyful co-adventurer in life. Thanks also to Thomas, Mollie, and Emilia, all of whom Mary Lou and I are so proud of, and who continue to bring much joy to us.

Appendix A—Additional Resources

See my website, **www.toolsforfeelingbetter.com**, for further information on (guess what?) tools for feeling better. Below are three additional excellent sources of books and other products:

1. Abraham-Hicks.com. Here you will find treasures of practical information for better daily living. Their work is transformative, and continues to inspire thousands to reconnect with their own inner joy.

2. karenmoneywilliams.com. Karen has had a remarkable impact on countless people for many years. Besides positively influencing friends and family locally and across continents, she is also the author of *It's a Beautiful Day in the Aber-hood* and is creator of the 40,000+ member Abraham Fun group on Facebook. Her magical words address the many small ways we can positively shift our energies in life.

3. goodvibeblog.com. Jeannette Maw has written extensively about the Law of Attraction, and her podcasts are a delight. See her website for books, her blog, and lots of joyful words.

Appendix B—The Advantages of the 10-Minute Practice

1. **The process focuses on practicing better feelings and it feels good to practice better feelings.** If someone said to me, "Do you think it would be worth it to sit down and do a little focusing for a bit, and then almost always feel better?" I think I would say yes to that.

2. **It is an easy process to do and 10 minutes/day is doable for most people.** Each day you can simply pick up the practicing tools and go.

3. **The practicing items are designed to be as "resistance-free" as possible.** This means that most of the practicing items are very general in nature (such as practicing a simple general good feeling about a topic). Our only goal is to find and practice better feelings for a topic, so that over time we simply get increasingly *used to* really good feelings about a topic.

4. **A large variety of tools are available to use in this practice.** There are many practicing items/tools in this book. Additionally, you can add your own tools from other sources. By having a large and varied set of tools to use in your practicing sessions, you can keep introducing new, fresh-feeling energy to any given topic.

Additionally, this allows you to identify favorite practicing items that you can then use with future topics.

5. **In the practicing, we are not obsessing over any one topic.** Since we focus on five topics in each 10-minute session, we are not obsessing over any one topic. This helps take the pressure off trying to find better feelings in any one area. Additionally, we focus on each topic for only two minutes per day. The idea is "get in, feel as good as you can, get out" (Abraham-Hicks).

6. **This is 10 minutes of good-feeling energy that you might not have otherwise had that particular day.** For me, this practice has ended up being a solid foundation/steadying-place within the many various, sometimes "crazy," events that occur in my life. Which leads us to another effect of doing this day after day…

7. **There is a remarkable cumulative effect of practicing better feelings for a specific topic, day after day.** In this practicing, we are gradually "growing and growing" better feelings in specific areas in our lives. So, over time, we tend to build powerful, positive-feeling momentum in those specific areas.

8. **This can be a key component in choosing/implementing a more proactive approach to practicing better energy in our lives.** In today's world, we are immersed in data, media, news, and events, and the more we can be *intentional* about choosing and growing good energies in our lives, the better.

About the Author

Rex has been a seeker of tools for better living all his life. In his thirties he partnered with a good friend, Rand Hoyt, to teach a series of classes called "The Things that Grab You in the Gut." Since then, while busy with his day job as a IT Analyst, Rex has continued to explore approaches for feeling better (and better) in life, resulting in this, his first book.

He lives with his wife, Mary Lou, in Orlando, Florida. They love having adventures with friends, going biking, and traveling. They especially enjoy visiting their son, daughter-in-law, and granddaughter in Dallas, Texas. Two dogs, Charlie and Broski, have recently found their way into Rex and Mary Lou's lives, which has added a whole lot of silliness to their household.

www.ingramcontent.com/pod-product-compliance
Lightning Source LLC
Chambersburg PA
CBHW071840080526
44589CB00012B/1061